THE
PAINTED
KITCHEN

THE
PAINTED
KITCHEN

Ideas and Inspiration for the Creative Home Decorator

CHARYN JONES

CASSELL

Cassell
Villiers House
41/47 Strand, London WC2N 5JE

Text © Charyn Jones 1992
Reprinted 1993 (twice)

First paperback edition 1993

Distributed in the United States by Sterling Publishing Co., Inc.
387 Park Avenue South, New York, NY 10016-8810

Distributed in Australia by Capricorn Link (Australia) Pty Ltd
P.O. Box 665, Lane Cove, NSW 2066

British Library Cataloguing-in-Publication Data
A catalogue record for this book is available from the British Library

ISBN 0–304–34236–X (Hardback)
ISBN 0–304–34390–0 (Paperback)

Paint Effects Photography: Susanna Price
Paint Effects: Plowden & Plowden

Typeset by RGM Associates, Lord Street, Southport

Printed and bound in Great Britain by Bath Colourbooks, Glasgow

CONTENTS

SECTION ONE

PLANNING
— FOR —
CHANGE

INTRODUCTION

Not many of us approach the redecoration of a room with a single-minded plan of action. Every room in a house, unless you are young or impecunious, has something in it that through thrift or sentiment you want to retain. So you will have to compromise or at least adapt when you go about setting a new style and redecorating. The kitchen is one of those rooms that matters a lot to some people but for others it is merely a functional laboratory for cooking. Indeed some people deliberately make their kitchens look like laboratories and spend great amounts of money doing it.

If the first rule is to build on what you have, the second must be to look carefully at what your tastes are. What are your ideas on colour and style? Do you want to reflect your personality or make a statement in a room where you may or may not be spending a lot of your time? The kitchen doesn't adapt too well to a rigid period setting. There is too much modern electrical equipment in even the most basic room for that. The kitchen today is a comparatively modern room; even the period farmhouse version, with an Aga and brick fireplace, will have items of modern technology such as the refrigerator/freezer.

Paint effects play a brilliantly successful role in turning the kitchen into your particular look – easily, cheaply and imaginatively. To help you plan and choose the colours and effects for your kitchen, *The Painted Kitchen* is divided into three sections: Section One offers a range of different kitchens with a great diversity of styles, from which you can select the ideas that appeal most to your particular taste. Section Two contains all the techniques you need to create the paint effects. There are no recipes to follow, and no rigid rules. No matter how experienced you are, you have to practise to find the best colour combinations and the best tools for the effect you want to achieve. The techniques have to be mastered before you start putting paint on the surface to be decorated. Section Three is devoted to the decorative detail: the items you can practise your paint effects on first before you attack something more major like walls, cupboards, floors or furniture.

Another planning consideration is the 'work triangle' – the shape made by the lines that connect the three main areas of activity in the kitchen. You usually walk from the food storage area (pantry and refrigerator) to the food preparation area (either kitchen table or worktop) to the cooking area (hob or oven). The total length of the three sides of this triangle represents how far you walk during typical cooking operations. If this is more than 7 m (23 ft) you will be giving yourself a lot of unnecessary walking.

There are also considerations about the height and width of the work surfaces. Most appliances and kitchen units are sold in a range of standard sizes. If you are not an 'average' size, or you want to make subtle adjustments, you can do so with different plinth heights or by raising the work surface by adding another layer. A serious cook, or one with a bad back, will probably lower the surface for bread and pastry making, and raise the height of the chopping board so that his or her back is straight when preparing foodstuffs. The hob can be lowered if you prefer to look into the saucepan during cooking.

PLANNING ON GRAPH PAPER

If you are starting the kitchen from scratch, plan the layout first on graph paper, using a suitable measurement to reduce everything to a manageable scale. Cut out the shapes of the appliances and place them on the measured-out diagram of the kitchen. Make sure you put in the correct sizes of the windows and other permanent structures, such as chimney breasts, doors and radiators. After the appliances are in place, draw the line between the fridge, the area where you are most likely to chop vegetables and prepare food, and the cooker. Measure the length of this triangle and convert it into real measurements. If it is more than 7 m (23 ft), you may have to consider repositioning, say, the cooker or fridge. While they should not be next to one another, they nevertheless should be fairly close so you don't spend too much time walking about the room with arms full of vegetables and other ingredients.

Other sensible rules need to be followed. If the cooking and preparation area are not adjacent and there is a throughway, carrying hot pans from one area to another with people or pets passing in and out could be dangerous.

Flamboyant yet traditional, this kitchen combines the old-world elements of solid-fuel cooking, a flagstone floor and the scrubbed wooden table of the farmhouse kitchen, with modern technology. Sensibly the latter has been hidden behind charmingly painted fascia panels to keep the traditional look intact.

THE KITCHEN AND ITS USES

The kitchen is primarily a room for cooking, but that is by no means its only function. If you are lucky enough to have a big room, then you can combine a number of other household activities in it if you want to. If you have young children, the kitchen is the place they invariably want to be when you are there too. So a corner for the children with a storage container for toys and an easily cleaned table is essential.

The kitchen is a sensible place to keep the household accounts and, rather than shoving them into a drawer, you could build in a small bureau with filing drawers and a desk top for other duties such as letter writing and so on. If the whole family, including teenage children, needs to use a computer, a large kitchen is possibly the most sensible place for it.

If you entertain a lot and don't pretend that the food arrives by magic, then the kitchen is *the* place for informal entertaining, and, of course, if you don't have a dining room, or feel that it might be used for something else, then a large kitchen can be visually divided to make a formal dining area too.

Historically, the kitchen was the centre of a bustling communal life; not only was food prepared there, as were the other seasonal activities of pickling and jam making, but it was a place where people could gather and feel warm. In today's cramped urban conditions, many kitchens are custom-built cubby holes where essential fixtures are slotted in and only one or two people can work without tripping over each other.

This is a well-planned functional kitchen. The L-shaped arrangement for the appliances means that the cook need not walk great distances. The table is placed in the centre of the floor with adequate space for visitors to sit without disturbing the cook.

ORGANIZING THE SPACE

If you are someone who thinks the kitchen is the centre of the house, and the existing kitchen is too small, then perhaps you could use another room for it or knock down a wall and make a more worthwhile space. The many permanent fixtures in a kitchen make it a difficult room to renovate piecemeal. It is quite often more cost effective to do it all at once and leave spaces for appliances such as dishwashers that may have to be purchased later. Once the plumbing is done and the tiles grouted you are not likely to uproot and change rooms if the one you have now is unsatisfactory. Whatever space you have, you will need to be realistic about what uses you can put it to. Whether or not you are a serious cook who requires a *batterie de cuisine* and a walk-in pantry, you still need to think seriously about the space and its allocation.

There are some useful technical guidelines about the way the work areas in a kitchen should be planned. These are mostly based on commonsense. The food preparation area should be near the knives. The pots and pans should be close to the oven and hob, and the plates and glasses should be in close proximity to the dishwasher and table.

DINING ROOMS

Eating in the kitchen is a daily occurrence but if you plan to entertain, there are ways of separating the space and making it feel and look different once the lights in the cooking area have been dimmed.

Lighting (see page 16) and ventilation are very important, especially in a kitchen where you eat on an informal and formal basis. If it suits your personality and style to entertain amongst the hurly burly of kitchen pots and ingredients, then it won't matter where the table is sited. If the room is wide, and the cooking and storage area are ranged along two opposite walls, then the only place for the table is down the centre of the room. This won't be an obstacle if one side is kept for the storage of crockery and cutlery so you don't have to pass back and forwards. The entire decorative scheme for such a room will need to be splendid – masses of china or glassware displayed on the dresser, and deep sinks and a dishwasher to get the mess out of sight. If the lighting is carefully placed under overhead cupboards, the work surface can be illuminated but not the room. Candles on the table would immediately make the table the focus of attention.

If you prefer to put the table at the end of a room, away from the cooking, then you can indulge in some soft furnishings, such as a floor rug, a trailing tablecloth and cushions on the chairs. This immediately softens hard edges and gives the appearance of comfort and relaxation.

If the room naturally splits into two distinct areas, the decoration can be completely different in each part, although there needs to be some consideration of continuity because both rooms will be visible simultaneously. If you want to keep the cooking area functional, then the dining area can be where you let your colour ideas run riot. An ornament or a splendid vase of flowers in an accent colour may be all that is needed.

The floor is the ideal surface on which to mark out a special dining area. Whether you decorate the floor with stencils, imitation parquet or marbling, you can plan carefully and divide the room into sections so that, say, a border separates out the part of the room intended for dining table and chairs. This visual trick gives formality to the dining area, just as a beautiful rug centred under the table will do.

If you are fortunate enough to have a kitchen that opens out onto a garden or patio area, the table can be placed close to the doors allowing the view to be enjoyed in cold weather and for the table to be moved outside when it is warm.

The table for such a dining area does not have to be a permanent fixture. A couple of trestles and boards, provided they are sturdy, will do, and they can be made as long or as short as you need. A tablecloth disguises the reality and they can be easily stored away, when not in use.

Dining areas can be matched to the kitchen units if you favour the overall look of kitchen company ranges. The dresser and table are colour washed in light yellow, with the decorative beading picked out in fine red lines. The paleness of the colour scheme makes a good backcloth for all forms of display and decoration, from dried flowers to house plants.

A ROOM FOR PLAY

Despite its creamy elegance, this kitchen has the easily washed surfaces and sturdy furniture appropriate for a room where toddlers may get into every corner. Safety catches should be installed on low-level doors and drawers.

The cheerful touches of repeating blue paint in this 'unfitted' kitchen are picked up by the floor stencils and the bright packaging of everyday groceries on the shelves. The gradations of blue from the dark ceiling downwards help to lower the height of the room.

While children are little, your life and theirs can be so much more comfortable if you plan for their space in the house and allow for their needs. No matter how well-appointed and well-planned a nursery room, young toddlers and children want to be near their parents. This obviously includes the kitchen where you spend so much time.

Traditionally children's play areas are decorated in bright primary colours. This can be copied in the corner of the kitchen designated as a play area. It may start out with an old-fashioned play pen for safety, if you have to leave the room, and eventually become equipped with a low-level work bench with storage units on castors. Ready-packed furniture now comes in so many clever styles that, for example, you can adapt wire laundry baskets on wheels for toy storage, which is then tucked away behind a cupboard door.

Kitchens are also the place where children's artwork can be shown off without spoiling the style. A square of soft board mounted on the wall can take the thumb tacks and saves marking the wall behind. Large floor cushions provide comfort for television watching. For many families, the child-centred decorative approach is often the one that dominates the rest of the room. So you may find yourself decorating the kitchen in a bright, cheerful way – perhaps using masking tape to split the colours or combing paint effects on the floors or furniture.

LIGHTING

Good lighting can make all the difference in any room. It creates mood and provides an essential function. It can show up a paint effect to advantage, so you need to plan the lighting carefully, rather than simply use what is there already. This is the area where few of us are experts and a little investment may be necessary. A day's work by an electrician in the kitchen is worth the expense – not only for fixing wall fittings and special lights for display and work surfaces, but also to ensure that all the electrical appliances are safely wired and switches are conveniently placed.

There is a vast range of lighting fittings and types of light available. The kitchen needs a number of different sorts. Fluorescent light is not kind to most complexions in a bathroom or bedroom but it is ideal for a work surface, particularly if the work surface is overlooked by cupboards where the slim tubes can be housed out of sight. The preparation area needs good strong light, if only to avoid accidents!

The sleek symmetry of this open-plan kitchen extends from the ceiling rafters to the glass-fronted storage cabinets on either end of the eating bar. The choice of plain light-coloured fittings further emphasizes the room's function as a room for working in, and helps create a feeling of spaciousness.

If you have any display shelving in the room, these take another sort of light – either directional from strategically placed spotlights or from lights attached beneath a plinth. You may also need a general purpose strong central light for everyday use to reduce the possibility of accidents. This may be an important component in your style, such as an elaborate old pendant light in a traditional kitchen or stainless steel functionalism in a modern room.

CREATING A MOOD

Once the practical lighting is taken care of, you can start to think about the mood. The cheapest and, in many ways, the most romantic option is natural candlelight. However, if you plan to use the kitchen as a dining area, or your style would look wrong with the dreamy romanticism of candles, then uplighters or downlighters are a good choice. These can be directed against the wall to reflect a softer light from the surface. They can also be placed so that the cooking and preparation areas are dimmed while you are eating.

It is probably safer and wiser not to use standard lamps in the kitchen, even in the dining area. Any trailing wires are doubly dangerous in areas with hot food and where slippery spills may occur.

The dining area is made to appear gloriously opulent with the choice of ochre colour-washed sponged walls and uplighters. The latter make ideal light fittings in any room, particularly if you fit dimmer switches. The lamp throws light directly on to the table.

VENTILATION

Ventilation and heating are important factors in a kitchen where the atmosphere can be cold and unwelcoming first thing in the morning and steaming hot while you are cooking. Warm moist air condenses on cold surfaces such as ceramic and glass. If the room is heated, this problem is reduced, but if you cook a lot then a hot and steamy room is not going to be comfortable. The best way of keeping the atmosphere in the kitchen fresh and controlled is with an extractor fan. This should be placed as high as possible in the room; the modern types can be cleverly integrated into the ceiling, wall or window. You can also have steam and smells extracted with a cooker hood sited directly above the hob. These can either be ducted through an outside wall, or recycle air, removing odours by means of a charcoal filter.

The extreme height in this narrow streamlined kitchen has been reduced to a less awesome level by an arched false ceiling and a frankly functional ventilation outlet above the cooking area. This allows the cook to use a modular charcoal grill unit on the hob.

COLOUR

Colours convey emotion and mood, and there are certain colours that are associated with certain styles. For example, a combination of different greens creates a cool atmosphere; gleaming white looks clean and efficient; and the country style nearly always includes a subtle pastel with natural earth colours. To be adventurous with colours, you need to understand them and this may involve trying something and being prepared to change it if it isn't right. For example, a sponged coat of apricot on a white base can be improved with a further coat of sponged pale green. You could keep going and spatter a deeper orange to finish off.

CHOOSING COLOURS

There are many ways of choosing colours, such as looking at pictures in books and magazines, and collecting paint colour cards. However, this is not the most satisfactory way of getting what you want. Colour reproduction is not always true to life and when the tin of paint is opened, it often looks nothing like you imagined from the colour card. Another approach is to try to understand the theory of colour and the way certain colours contrast or blend with others. This is often understood best by looking at the colour wheel. For example, if you want a colour to contrast with another, you look at the opposite colour in the wheel, such as yellow and purple, red and green. If you opt for a safer scheme and you want a colour to blend or harmonize, then look at those spokes of colour that are adjacent to your chosen colour, such as blue and green, or orange and yellow.

Because paint effects are essentially about mixing colours together, you will need a clear idea of what you like before you start. You may have a favourite colour, but what would it look like painted over an expanse of wall? How will the natural and artificial light in the room treat the colour? How will colours react with each other; will they change dramatically when placed side by side? You will need to look at the colour scheme as a whole.

PSYCHOLOGY OF COLOUR

The psychology of colour is something that is considered by marketing executives, advertising directors and interior designers. Colour schemes for the years ahead are carefully planned and promoted through fashion and technology. Look at the cars on the street and notice how the bright colours of five years ago have been replaced by pearlized serious shades. It is a good idea for you too to think about your responses to colour so that when you redecorate you can analyse what your preferences are and why.

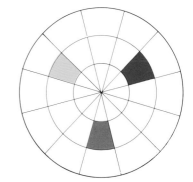

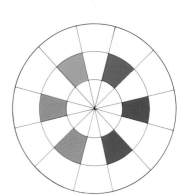

The colour wheel can be used to understand the theory of colour.

Most of us know what colours we like instinctively, but may never question our reasons. If you look in your wardrobe, you may find that you stick to certain colours and avoid others. Perhaps you have a monochrome wardrobe but add colour with accessories. If this is the way you want to approach your kitchen walls and cupboards, then think about a neutral background, perhaps a pale green colour wash, with displays of china or brightly coloured table linen as the spashes of colour.

Another consideration before you start on a colour scheme relates to the size and position of the room (see pages 26–27). If you need to change the perception of the room's size, you may have to consider using certain tones of colour – darker for a large cavernous room or lighter for a small room with a low ceiling. The amount of natural light that enters the room and how bright the room is, and for how long, are other matters that need thinking about. A bright white room will be startling if it gets the sun all day, whereas a pastel tone will give a more restful feel. Daylight is the time to judge a colour scheme, as artificial lighting can trick the eye and produce all sorts of shifts of light. In the harsh light of day, your colours and surfaces will be exposed.

The colour wheel is made up of the purest intense colours – like a rainbow. Those colours alongside your chosen colour will blend harmoniously with it; for a bolder approach, the colours opposite will contrast and provide a more dazzling effect.

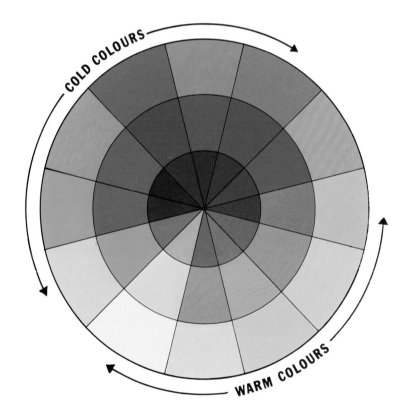

COLD COLOURS

WARM COLOURS

SENSE OF FUN

When approaching colour choices, relax and have some fun. Too often kitchens are created solely as working areas where storage units are placed around electrical appliances. A more positive stance will reap unexpected benefits. You can take one of two approaches; you can start with a style, and use the accepted colour schemes associated with it. For example, the French Provençal style uses the hot sunny colours of the Mediterranean – terracotta, blue, chrome yellow and rusty pink. Or you can start with one or two of the colours you like and enjoy living with. With this option you can acknowledge the technology in the kitchen, adding colour and individualism with decorative details (see Section Three).

The designer of this distinctly modern kitchen, with its irregular lines and large blocks of colour, has chosen to contrast warm red and yellow with their opposites on the colour wheel – green and lilac pink.

The final decision is whether you are going all the way with a chosen style or whether you will build the décor up gradually, experimenting as you go. This latter approach may sound more reasonable, but the essential thing to remember is unity. Nothing succeeds if there isn't a unity of purpose and application. The simplest system is to use one colour for the walls, floor and ceiling, or you may end up with a medley of colours and styles that will leave you dissatisfied and annoyed that you didn't plan more carefully. Few people have such a clear overview without forethought.

FITTING THE COLOURS TO THE ROOM

The cool colours are sensible for a room where the sun pours in for most of the day. They are also reputed to induce calm. These colours include greens, blues and violets. Grey and white can also appear cool. A high-tech style of kitchen is often decorated in cool colours to complement the stainless steel, chrome, shiny appliances and ceramic tiles.

The vibrant red colour wash and the neo-classical motifs in the kitchen opposite help to create a unity of approach. The appliances are hidden behind fascia panels and the elegant table setting doesn't look out of place in this workroom for cooking and eating in (see page 108).

The designer of this kitchen has taken the classical colours of Pompeii as a starting point. Shades of red and grey have been ragged over the kitchen cupboard doors (see page 72). The colour scheme is cool and stylish, a feature echoed by the marbled floor.

Warm colours are ideal for a room that sees little sun and where the ceiling is high, making the room appear lofty and impersonal. The warm colours are the reds, yellows and oranges. They are the exciting colours that are supposed to make us move and work faster.

Pastels are easy to live with. They are colours to which white has been added. They can also be boring if used without any accent or statement. The 'dull' colours are those that have black added. They are more unusual and some have associations with nature – the colours of lichens, plums and grapes, for example.

A practical way of choosing colours that 'go' together is to pick up items, such as a terracotta flower pot, the petal of a favourite flower, or a piece of china and try to match colours in this way with found objects that you have a positive emotional response to. Leave them lying about in the kitchen and assess your responses to them. With these objects, and pictures of the style, colour cards, sample paint boards (see page 61) and swatches of fabric, you can start to plan the colour scheme and see how the colours react with one another and in the room.

SOME UNBEATABLE SCHEMES

Warm apricot paint covers almost every surface – shelves, doors and ceiling. Because texture has been added with honey-coloured wood and gleaming stainless steel, the scheme succeeds, despite the uniformity.

Neutral colour schemes don't have to be boring. You can add texture in the form of coir matting, cork tiles, linen curtains or table linen, and textured paint effects such as marbling and combing.

A monochrome scheme works well in a kitchen because the electrical appliances are usually gleaming white. If you use white, off-white or grey and choose subtle complementary colours, you can't go wrong. You can even bring in some of the baroque colours in dull tones, such as the dusty maroons and purples of dried flowers.

White with one accent colour, if adhered to strictly, makes a strong statement. For example, a pristine white kitchen might have a border of tiles in blue or green, as well as the wooden skirting, dado rail and window surrounds.

However, you don't need to recreate the tried and tested formula, this is your chance to try something truly individual. Have fun mixing colours first. Use old tins of paint and mix them in with one another (see page 58). By a process of trial and error you will soon learn what works and what doesn't.

The best paint base colour to start from is an off-white eggshell or emulsion. To that add some colour and if it is too bright, add more white to soften it into a pastel or paler shade or add black to dull it. Then test your colours on a piece of lining paper or plaster board. When colour dries, it is not as bold as when wet. Make notes as you go. Use the tubes of artist's oils or powder colours for fine tuning. Raw umber, essential when mixing colours where you want an ageing effect (see page 96), mellows any colour. Try different effects by dividing up your base into a number of smaller containers and adding different colours to each to see the best result for you. These samples can then form the basis for a paint effect.

STYLE

Colour and paint effects can be used to change perceptions about the proportions of a room. For example, if your kitchen has a high ceiling which tends to make it seem rather large and unfriendly, you can induce cosiness by painting the ceiling in a darker shade than the walls. Choose your ceiling colour with care if the rest of the room has a strong colour scheme otherwise you could end up with a cavernous effect instead – oppressive and dull. On the other hand, colours that reflect light open out the space so a light ceiling and pale-coloured walls in a low room prevents a claustrophobic feeling, making the room seem airier and larger.

A more deliberate effect is to lighten the wall colour gradually as you approach the ceiling – say stippling, colourwashing or sponging in bands of paler shades up the wall. A pale colour scheme to give the feeling of space doesn't have to be treated in one effect only. Try one pale paint effect on the walls, with a white marbled floor and monochrome cupboards.

The shapes and colours of a sunny climate create the style for this kitchen. The colour-washed green on the walls provides a relaxing background to the beautifully crafted wooden units. The ventilation hood over the hob is disguised as a sunburst and even the plinth hasn't escaped the designer's eye for detail.

If the room is long and narrow, use geometry to trick the eye into thinking it is wider. This can be done on the floor with a clever use of floor tiles or, in keeping with our theme, with a *trompe l'oeil* of marbled or fake marquetry lozenges or diamonds, elongated across the narrow width to make the space appear to open out. A plain border that follows the skirting and the plinth panels on the kitchen units will visually confine the squares or diamonds to the central area. Use graph paper and coloured pens to plan any visual tricks carefully before you start.

STRUCTURAL FEATURES

Another way to alter proportion and perspective in a room is to use the structural features or, where there are none, to put some in. Large expanses of wall can be broken up in the traditional way with a dado or chair rail. This is placed 1 m (39 in) above the floor (where the chair back would scrape the wall if it were placed up against it). These rails are usually made from wooden or plaster mouldings, but a similar effect can be achieved with a simple strip of colour. Using paint effects, this band could be marbled or stencilled, or it can be a simple *trompe l'oeil* line, such as *grisaille*, in which grey lines are used to fake relief.

There are many ways of breaking up the flat areas in the wall space between dado and skirting boards to add architectural interest and detail. Tongue and groove panelling is available in many different designs, either plain or with pronounced bevelled edges. These wooden fillets give a sense of age and permanence, and they provide good insulation too. Panels can be painted to look like better quality wood (see page 90), limed (see page 94) or aged in traditional colours (see page 96).

A plain plastered wall can be divided up into sections with lines instead of wooden mouldings; stencils are quite often placed like a border just above the skirting board, where there is already a straight line, or in place of the dado. The decoration beneath the dado can become a unifying feature if the cupboard doors are treated in the same way. This creates a sameness which would suit a tidy kitchen where everything has it place.

Further up the wall, a high ceiling can be lowered by blurring the junction between ceiling and wall. If the ceiling is sponged or colourwashed, you can continue this effect down to picture-rail height. The picture rail is another conventional divider in the classical proportions of a room. In the cornice area, stencils or another decorative edging can add depth to the wall if necessary, and they will certainly add interest if the wall is large and featureless.

Picture-rail level, unless you want to hang pictures in the kitchen, is a useful place to position a shelf where decorative and rarely used china or earthenware can be stored. If the ceiling isn't high, the pot shelf can be used as the Shakers in America used it – as a place from which to hang pots and other essential items.

With fantasy effects you can alter even more than the basic dimensions of a room, you can create a whole new style. For example, if your kitchen is

furnished with laminated units from a chain store, you can sand them down and paint them in keeping with the style of the room. Make the cheap pine dresser look as if it is an antique, with the wear and tear of generations of use. The floor can be stained in lozenge shapes like parquet to resemble the floor of a stately home.

CHOOSING THE COLOURS

Styles go in and out of fashion and get little attention until a designer chooses the colours and motifs of a particular style and popularizes it. So in recent years styles reminiscent of Provence in the south of France and the ecclesiastical shapes and images of Gothic have been in vogue – Provençal with its vibrant sun-drenched colours and teardrop motifs and Gothic with carved wood and cream and pastels. As there are as many styles as there are civilizations, there is no shortage to choose from. The problem for the amateur is to keep the motifs and colours to one style and to avoid muddling them. That does not mean you cannot opt for an eclectic mix – a combination of sympathetic styles.

The choice of green as the accent colour and the gleaming enamelled surfaces of the appliances and the glass light fittings give a soft country-style look to the kitchen opposite. Brick and wood help to add texture.

Pink is always pretty, and so is the kitchen below. The approach is consistent – the stencil is repeated on the cupboards and drawers, on the floor and on the painted wooden chairs. Wallpaper in a more vibrant pink covers the walls, and the large window gives a sense of space, making this a light, sociable kitchen.

THE PERIOD OF THE HOUSE

Whatever you do to any room in your house, it is a good rule to try to keep in style with the other rooms. This does not necessarily mean slavishly copying the style of the period of the house you live in, although the structure of your home should be respected. Victorian houses, for example, with their clutter and darkened rooms, don't always suit our modern way of life. With kitchens there is usually not much room for extensive architectural features such as mouldings and ornamental plasterwork. If the kitchen has a fireplace, for example, it may not be practical to leave it there as the space left by the fireplace is usually deep enough for storage cupboards. Equally, if more of the chimney breast is cut away, a microwave can be set into the brickwork.

A large part of the kitchen is dominated by the need for cupboards and shelves. These kitchen units can be used to imitate the style of the house. Styles of mouldings, brass door knobs, floral stencils on door panels and aged wood all evoke particular periods and styles.

STYLE DETAIL

To be original, you can pick up a motif and paint effect that conjure up a particular time and place. Symbols of ancient Rome might be amphora vases, terrazzo tiles and distressed plasterwork. Regency and Georgian interior design, with their classical proportions and panelling, give an air of elegance and restrained grandeur. You can take elements from these eras and have some fun with them, rather as a stage-set designer would.

For an elegant effect, you will need a large room with tall windows and graceful proportions. If not, compromise with some additional mouldings around the door and window frames, and deepen the skirting board with another layer of moulding. You could reduce the flat surfaces and add more texture or ornamentation with glazing in the cupboard doors, so that the glassware and china can be shown off. Stencilling in neo-classical motifs also looks elegant. The floors can be plain boards with stained areas to resemble parquet flooring. The walls can be finished like Regency stripes using masking tape and a silky finish, such as dragging or combing (see pages 82 and 84).

Gothic is another fashionable style that depends on religious architectural shapes, drapes and table linen in swathes of linen or muslin, large dripping candles, fake leading on glass and a paint effect, like whitewashed walls.

The end of the nineteenth century brought many new styles that are favourites in the kitchen because of their celebration of functionalism and

Not for the technologically minded, the human scale of this kitchen conjures up images of farmhouse cottages of centuries ago. The atmosphere of the period has been lovingly recreated with the appropriate furniture, sympathetic materials and the all-important focal point of the old coal-burning range.

natural materials and shapes. The Arts and Crafts and the Art Nouveau movements are much more accessible because the motifs and colours are instantly recognizable. You can be sure visitors will recognize your attempts at theatre if you introduce the motifs of the Art Nouveau school, for example, with some stained glass (see page 126) or displays of china from the period.

The country look in kitchens is much influenced by early American farmhouse kitchens, with hand-crafted furnishings and folk art on the walls, as well as cheerful painted furniture with natural colours, or scrubbed wood and colour washed walls. There needs to be a focal point, however. If there is no Aga or hearth, then the kitchen table with the paraphernalia of family life can provide a focus. Other details are the rocking chair, gingham table cloths and pot shelves or a corner cupboard with stencilled motifs, and traditional handmade rag rugs on the floor.

A more English-style country look can be achieved with florals and sprigs, an air of informality and natural materials. Perhaps the emphasis here is on prettiness – flowers and displays of china and homemade jams, rag-rolled woodwork in pastel colours. Or you could attempt a flowing decorative style with your own block painting that continues over walls, doors and even onto the curtains (see page 104).

CONTEMPORARY LOOKS

Modern styles are not so difficult to achieve; it is the essential elements that are more important. Clutter is put away out of sight with one or two well-designed pieces acting as token ornamentation – perhaps an Italian expresso coffee maker or an elegant juice squeezer. Colour can be introduced with stripes or brightly combed floorboards. As long as the treatment isn't fussy, paint effects such as marbling and wood graining fit well into the modern kitchen. Alternatively try a monochrome combination like grey or black with a little white, grey on grey combing or a watered silk finish which is achieved by two-directional dragging or combing (see page 84).

For a basic kitchen, where the pipes have not been chased into the plasterwork, don't pretend they aren't there. Emphasize them instead by painting them in bright colours or in the colours of industrial-type materials such as aluminium and steel.

DECISION TIME

All this assumes that you are lucky enough to start from scratch with no real constraints except budget and space. In fact, for most of us, some form or compromise is required in finding a style and trying to integrate it with what is already there. This is made easier nowadays by the kitchen unit manufacturers who provide fascia panels that fit over the electrical appliances. So, if you have inherited bright orange laminated units, don't despair. You can rub down laminate, and even melamine, finishes. Once primed, they can be painted with any effect.

We nearly all have something we have inherited or something that is too good to throw away. So we have to adapt. Focus on the best parts. The department store dresser in bright pine can be distressed to fit in with a Scandinavian scrubbed white floor or painted a dark green and embellished with folk art stencils in primary colours. The pine can be wood grained to resemble age-old oak for an elegant dinner setting. A spectacular display area can be created from an oversized chest or cupboard: glaze the doors and display your glass and china, or collect attractive packaging for your dry goods. Paint the cupboard the same as the walls so it looks 'built-in'. And if you don't like the style of a piece, such as a large mass-produced kitchen unit, reduce the ugliness of any prominent mouldings by painting the whole piece in one effect – dragging or sponging. The unpleasant proportions will be absorbed into the new appearance of the whole.

You could even change the appearance of the appliances. It is perfectly possible to paint metal in a range of stylish finishes (see page 52). An old but serviceable fridge could be given a fun treatment – it certainly looks better if you don't pretend that it is a professional job. Then add accessories to suit the style (see Section Three).

This kitchen has a contemporary feel with its flowing lines and attractive materials. The designer has revelled in materials that can be used in a sinuous way. The stainless steel ventilator hood is curved over the hob; the granite worktop is gently rounded off to provide a work surface; nowhere is a sharp edge to be seen. Colour choice is, however, more traditional – red and blue dragged wood and tartan fabric.

WALLS AND CEILINGS

The walls and ceiling present the largest surfaces in the room. They are the areas where you can play around with perspective and space. They also attract the dirt and grease which are inevitable in a room where there are fluctuating changes in atmosphere.

Paint effects are the ideal tools here in the kitchen. However, you need to consider all the other surfaces simultaneously. The whole effect will be diminished if you ignore part of the room. That isn't to say that every exposed surface should be treated with a paint effect, but it should be treated with an eye for the dimensions and style of the room.

CEILINGS

This kitchen benefits from solid ancient beams and the paintwork has been tactfully aged with paint effects to complement them. A careful choice of accessories – the cast-iron candelabra, copper pots and pans and swathes of fabric – help to maintain the old fashioned look and create a convivial atmosphere.

The ceiling is the place to start and it is also the surface that we most frequently disregard and end up painting in a plain colour. Paint can be used to improve the proportions of the room. If the ceiling is high, and this height isn't compatible with the chosen style, then it needs to be painted a darker colour to lower the height. Conversely, if the ceiling is low, then paint it cream or white and carry the colour down onto the walls – to the height of the picture rail. If you live in a modern house with no ornamentation, such as a cornice or picture rail, then a painted stripe or a stencil can do the trick and improve the proportions of the room by imitating mouldings.

As it is difficult and uncomfortable to paint ceilings, you may decide to settle for a roller and emulsion paint. The memories of blue clouds scudding across the ceiling and twinkling stars may send shudders down your spine, but a soft colourwashed finish in pale pastel colours produces a light, ethereal effect, and if you continue this down the wall to picture-rail height, the sharp line where ceiling meets wall will disappear.

The major consideration when choosing paint for the ceiling is that the surface can be cleaned easily. Hot air rises and any dust and grease is then trapped on the ceiling. Emulsion is the best choice because gloss or silk finishes will show up any imperfections in the plasterwork.

Sponging or colourwashing are good techniques for the ceiling because they are not difficult to do and you can stop for a while to consider where more colour needs to go or whether to lighten or darken its intensity.

For problem ceilings where the surface is pitted and scarred, you may need to paper with a lining paper or a relief wallpaper, and either stipple the surface to age it or colourwash it with a tint of raw umber to imitate the Victorian glazed look. The ceiling can also be used to hang decorative flowers or basketware or an interesting light fitting, such as a candelabra.

BEAMS

For houses with beams, the kindest treatment is a soft finish of beeswax or linseed oil. Beams are the perfect prop for kitchen paraphernalia – dried flowers and herbs, hanging baskets and a *batterie de cuisine*. If you put in new beams, then wood graining (see page 90), combing (see page 84) or liming (see page 94) will age them in hours. If there are too many beams and they overpower the room, making it seem claustrophobic, it may be wiser to paint them the same colour as the ceiling, leaving untouched those embedded in the wall or over the fireplace to show off the mellowed wood.

In the tiny kitchen opposite, a warm, cosy atmosphere is created with yellow colour-washed surfaces and a tiny stencilled motif.

WALLS

Unless you have a large kitchen, there probably won't be as much wall space to decorate as in other rooms in the house. Wall storage cupboards, tall fridges and eye-level ovens cover much of the wall up to at least 2 m (6 ft 6 in). Nevertheless the walls need to be treated as sympathetically as possible to fit in with the age of the house and the style or period you have chosen. This is particularly important if you have a lot of gleaming appliances.

The minimalist kitchen below is both functional and exciting. The clever choice of blocks of colour in shades of purple to off-set the gleaming white appliances makes a bold statement. Cool colours such as purple and blue complement shining metal surfaces.

If you have chosen a country style, for example, then you do not need to ensure a pristine smooth plaster finish on the walls; the more 'natural' the surface the better. You can even apply a filler at random, sand it and recreate a rustic country wall. A colourwashed finish will complete the farmhouse look. If your kitchen is high-tech, the walls may need to be skimmed to get a perfect plaster finish. Whatever the paint finish, you will need to seal it with some form of varnish (see page 61) to protect your handiwork and to maintain a washable surface.

Ceramic tiles are a practical choice near sinks because they provide an impermeable surface. Tiles are now available in so many colours and designs that you need to choose carefully to maintain the unity of your decorative scheme. With everything available from Aztec and Delft colours to gingham and trellis all-over patterns, you may be tempted to go overboard. If you choose too bold a design, however, the wall decoration will suffer by comparison, so take care.

The spaces between the tiles are also a design feature. Large spaces with white or coloured grouting look more rustic, whereas an all-over soft pastel sprig pattern with narrow grouting gives a more seamless finish. Alternatively, you could create your own mosaic of broken tiles. Grouting also comes in colours other than white and neutral.

SYMPATHETIC MATERIALS

Wood panelling can be designed to suit a style or to provide a disguise if the plasterwork is not perfect. Panelling between the skirting board and the dado rail is a traditional feature and can be easily done by even an inexperienced carpenter. Tongue and groove panelling comes in many different styles, some of them highly elaborate. The boards interlink and can be nailed or screwed to battens arranged at intervals horizontally across the wall. A moulding at the top finishes off the effect neatly.

Sheets of plywood can be turned into fake panelling with masking tape and monochrome paint. You can build up a three-dimensional moulding by painting lines to represent the wood, the moulded edges and the shadows (see page 00). There are now many commercial mouldings and materials that can create panelling to match cupboard doors. Select from a plain or moulded dado rail or skirting boards and combine them with plywood to form panels. The ply and mouldings can then be distressed by dragging, liming or staining (see pages 82, 94 and 138).

In a well-equipped kitchen there may be so little free wall space that a short length of dado looks isolated. In those circumstances, the best idea may be to replace it with a utility moulding such as a Shaker-style peg board for oven gloves, children's aprons or kitchen utensils.

The *tour de force* in the kitchen is the *trompe l'oeil* effect (see page 106) – a bowl of vegetables on the splashback, garlic and onion garlands, a vase of flowers and pots and pans. Have fun, the uniformity of kitchen appliances cries out for an irreverent approach.

FLOORS

When considering effects for the kitchen floor, take into account that it is likely to be subjected to much wear and tear, particularly around the preparation, storage and cooking areas, and it will be spattered with water, food and grease. It must also be able to withstand frequent cleaning and be non-slip for safety.

If your kitchen is large enough to divide into two distinct areas – one for cooking and the other for eating – you don't have to be so utilitarian in the dining part. You can design and execute a work of art or scatter with rugs.

The floor provides a surface where you can play around with perspective, changing the apparent dimensions of the room. For example, in a small square room, if you lay tiles or paint a diamond grid on the floor on the diagonal, starting from the door, the eye will be drawn into the distance, making the room appear longer. If the room has a neutral coloured floor with no focal point, there will be nothing else to catch the eye – there is usually no furniture in the centre of the kitchen work area – and the effect may be dull. However, if your kitchen is hard working and sleek, this no-frills austerity may be just the effect you are after.

The gleaming varnished cork provides a warm and sympathetic flooring material in this functional kitchen with its open shelving. Cork has a reputation as a mellow, warm surface, offsetting the harshness of cooler-looking china and enamel surfaces.

MATERIALS

While modern vinyl, ceramic and linoleum floor surfaces have all the qualities essential for kitchens, one of the best floors for paint effects is the one that may already be there – natural wood floorboards. They can take many different finishes, providing a perfect grid for stencils and imitation flooring effects. Concrete is a cheap and cheerful flooring and there are special concrete paints which make any finish possible.

With floorboards, semi-transparent wood stains allow the natural grain of the wood to be seen and the range isn't just wood coloured – there are pastels, jewel colours and brights too. They can provide the decoration alone or be the background colour for a decorative stencil.

Wood stains are available on their own or combined with a varnish. As it is quite difficult to control the intensity of the colour, you might decide to colour first and apply protective varnish when the intensity is right. A coat of varnish on its own will show up any flaws in the wood, so for old floorboards you might have to stain or bleach the boards before varnishing. If you thin the varnish for the first two coats, this makes application easier.

Preparation is essential. You will almost certainly need to sand old boards with a hired sanding machine to remove dirt, grime, old varnish and nail

Stencilling in soft muted colours works well on stripped, scrubbed floorboards. The latter offer a perfect grid when planning the design. This stencil design combines large poppy motifs with the geometric lines of braids and herringbone patterns.

marks. (If the boards don't need this level of sanding, simply go over them with sandpaper.) Any large cracks should be filled with fillets of wood to fit the space snugly. If the boards are very bad, plywood sheets cut to fit provide a level, stable surface for decorative finishes. As the wood will have to be cut into pieces to fit the room, you could make a feature of this by cutting them into squares and use the joins as a feature.

PLANNING A DESIGN

Use a piece of graph paper to make up a floor plan to scale. Fill in the spaces taken up with appliances and storage, and any tables or other items. You can get inspiration for lozenge or fake marble effects from advertisements for modern floorings or you can imitate traditional floors such as the parquet and elaborate marquetry of stately homes. Though the idea of painting or staining separate boards may sound rather limiting, by choosing a geometric pattern where a series of stripes is bound by a square, and using wood tints or stains, you can get an authentic-looking floor.

The parquet idea has many possibilities. Combine honey colours with dark ebony and chestnut brown in clever geometry. You will need to plan this carefully using graph paper to scale. Colour the squares in with pencils or watercolours to represent the patterns.

As long as you feel confident about your ability to execute the paint effect, the fact that it is being created on the floor shouldn't be a major obstacle. It is a relatively easy surface to decorate with paint, provided your knees and back can stand the strain and you prepare the surface properly! For their durability oil-based paints are the best choice but emulsion will give you a wide range of colours, particularly if you only plan to rub colour into the boards. Whatever the paint, the surface will have to be protected with four coats of varnish.

To transfer the design onto the floor, you can use masking tape to show where lines should intersect or where motifs are placed.

EFFECTS

Paint effects that work well on floorboards are liming (see page 94), and stencilling (see page 99) – whether borders, all over patterns or isolated motifs. Choose colours from the rest of the room decoration. Stencils all over or around the perimeter can be applied after staining; use stains or diluted paint. Wood stains make particularly good stencil paints on floors. A trick to remember is to score along the outlines beforehand so that the paint doesn't seep over onto the other colours. The entire floor must then be carefully sealed against water and wear and tear.

For both plywood and floorboards try a combed effect either in a wood colour or a completely unlikely one to go with your scheme, or work up a marbled floor imitating tiles or an Italian palazzo. Don't forget the skirting boards; they should continue the theme. Marbling can be planned in the same way as fake parquet. Divide the floor up into squares; this makes the planning and execution easier and also means that the floor looks less like sheet vinyl. You can paint stripes all around the edge and even diamonds at the corners of each square.

For the seriously artistic, a fake floorcloth provides an interesting focal point in that part of the kitchen where you eat or watch television. You should map out the design first and then use any technique you wish to build up an interesting imitation rug.

Block painting, for those less sure of their freehand abilities, ensures a regular pattern and if you choose your colours carefully and seal the work with lots of coats of varnish to give it depth, the design will last for a long time. This is particularly suitable for the floor with poor boards. When they are painted, if the colours look brassy and bright, they can always be dulled or aged with a wash of eggshell and raw umber diluted with four parts solvent and then lightly sanded before applying the varnish to protect the painted finish.

Hot earth colours scud across the dining area of this large New Mexican-style kitchen. The radiator is similarly sponged as a disguise. The theme is maintained by the choice of objects – the candlesticks and the hot colours of the floral and fruit display. A touch of azure blue provides a cooler note.

WORKTOPS

In a dream kitchen, different work surfaces are designed for different demands. The end-grain wood butcher's block is set in specially for the preparation of meat and vegetables; ceramic tiles top the area where hot pans are taken direct from the hob or oven; a marble or granite slab is installed for pastry making. In reality work surfaces are not usually set out like that unless you are lucky enough to be starting from scratch.

All food preparation areas in the kitchen should be waterproof. Stainless steel and ceramics are the most reliable impermeable surfaces. However, wood is now a real favourite for kitchen worktops because of its warmth; although softer, any scratches seem to enhance its attractiveness. But if you choose wood, you must seal it thoroughly to protect against water, food juices and smells.

The ideal kitchen has a work surface for every need. Here granite provides a heat-resistant surface adjacent to the hob; the wooden central work table is made up from ash, granite and end-grain maple – providing pastry making and food preparation surfaces.

HARD OR SOFT

Woods are classified according to the type of tree they come from. Hardwoods are from trees with broad leaves, and softwoods from coniferous trees. The concern at the destruction of the tropical rainforest where many of the beautiful hardwoods are grown (mahogany and teak) has resulted in many people trying to use the more sustainable woods grown in temperate zones. These include oak, beech, cherry and elm and the softwoods such as yew and pine.

Any worktop wood should be sealed to prevent it drying out and splitting. There are many finishes for wood to make it easier to clean and to help keep up its appearance. These are the soft finishes of wax and oil and the hard finishes of French polish, shellac and varnish. Wax and oils are somewhat impractical for the kitchen as they are not very durable; although the surface has a lustrous sheen, it will be marked by heat and will get dirty easily. French polish is a high-gloss finish that is usually found on fine pieces of furniture such as tables and cabinets. Shellac is a product used in French polishing but it is best used for decorative areas because it will not withstand water or heat.

Any surface in frequent contact with water must be varnished. This is the toughest finish and is easy to look after. The widely available all-purpose polyurethane varnishes are now the most common choice. They come in gloss, semi-gloss and matt finishes. The first two or three coats can be thinned for easier application; four coats is really the minimum for a truly waterproof finish. Check with the manufacturer if you are uncertain and observe the rules about drying times. The surface must be clean, dry and dust-free before you start and you need to use special varnish brushes for the job (see page 63).

The range of treatments for wood on worktops to enhance its natural beauty include liming, staining and subtle pale stencils. Wood stains allow the natural grain to show through and they can be used for the stencilling. As long as you prepare the surface well and take time and effort over your work, a marbled or imitation stonework paint effect will fool anyone. These painterly effects need to be protected with up to 8–10 coats of varnish to prevent them being short lived.

The mahogany worktop and the pine table are the focal point in this luscious creamy kitchen, very much in the grand style. Wooden surfaces must be carefully prepared with either varnish or oils to give a life-time of use. The sink has been cleverly installed using a solid old table as a base.

TABLE TOPS

Although the kitchen table often needs to be used as an extra worktop, you can really use your imagination to decorate it with paint. If your table isn't up to being restored to resemble a refectory table of great antiquity, then settle for a paint effect. Study the lines of the table – even the heaviest legs and most solid top can be transformed with a careful paint finish.

Think of some of the exotic treatments given to coffee tables for your inspiration. During the day any paintwork can be protected by a laminated table cloth. There is no reason why a kitchen table shouldn't be painted in a mellow pale yellow and gold with a stylized stencil around the perimeter, or try a fantasy finish like malachite. Spattering (see page 80) in bold colours on a neutral background also looks wonderful.

STORAGE UNITS

A fitted kitchen, where everything matches and appliances can be hidden away behind identical panels, is a disadvantage if you inherit one with a finish that you don't like or one that doesn't fit with the style or period you have chosen. It is possible to change the overall style of an existing kitchen, but this depends very much on the materials and surfaces in place.

Plastic laminates and melamine are practical, easy-to-clean surfaces but they are not easy to change. Any alteration to the colour will inevitably spoil the finish because the surface has to be rubbed down in order to provide a key for the paint medium. This isn't a problem on the front panels but there are usually narrow facings on the edges, and these are less easy to enhance successfully. Even wooden kitchens may not be all they seem. The cupboard doors may be wood veneer rather than solid wood, and it is difficult to change veneer without damaging it.

When a kitchen is installed in an irregular space, innovative ideas for storage become a necessity. Here long shelving provides display and essential storage for those items that are difficult to put into cupboards. This form of display is ideal for the lazy cook where those items that are used regularly are to hand at all times.

DRESSERS

Dressers and sideboards have long provided useful kitchen storage and there is little doubt that in the right position they are both practical and attractive. They enhance the appearance of the kitchen and make a good focal point.

A dresser does not have to be an antique; it can easily be custom built to fit a room. At its simplest it is a sideboard with wooden shelves above and drawers and/or cupboards beneath or a chest of drawers topped with some shelves in the same wood or colour scheme. The drawers are the only complex joinery.

You can create an authentic farmhouse style for a dresser by making a backing with tongue and groove boards. Or you can continue the wall paint behind – but choose carefully because if you plan to display china and glass on the dresser shelves, the combination of paintwork and lighting needs to be thought about carefully or the display could merge with its background.

Dressers were originally made from fine hardwood, but with the trend in reproduction furniture, there are now reasonable dressers to be had in many different woods, shapes and sizes. Traditional treatments such as blue and

Dressers come in all shapes and sizes and this aged dresser has been arranged so the shelving section is wall-mounted above the sturdy old-fashioned base. The cream paintwork stands out well against the deep colour of the wall.

green (see page 96) dragged and limed wood are replacing the stripped pine look. There is no end to the embellishments for a dresser – stencils across the top fascia panel and on the drawers around the knobs, painted cupboard doors, delicate lines along the shelf edges and a contrast colour picked out around the moulding (see page 12).

CUPBOARDS

Good preparation and a tough surface are essential because the cupboard doors are going to be subjected to much wear and tear. The surface needs rubbing down between each successive coat. Laminate should be well washed first to remove grease and immediately sanded with wet and dry paper while it is still wet. Wash and dry again before applying the paint.

The prepared surface is usually primed, undercoated, then given two top coats of paint, the decorative finish and then a protective varnish. Rub down between coats with finer and finer grades of abrasive paper. To prevent scratching, use wet and dry paper. As several thin coats of paint build up a better finish than fewer thicker ones, thin the paint with the appropriate thinner (see page 61) to a ratio of about 3:1. Cupboards are usually painted in gloss, but you will get a more interesting finish if you use eggshell or emulsion in satin/silk finishes and then create a shine using varnish.

Some paint effects are particularly popular for kitchen cupboards. Dragging (see page 82), stippling (see page 74) and sponging (see page 70) are not difficult to do yourself and spattering (see page 80), though not easy on vertical surfaces, can be controlled on the smaller area of a door, particularly if you can take the doors off.

If the doors have a beading panel, the beading can be picked out in another colour and the centre of the panel painted with a different effect or even a fantasy finish. If the doors have no special features, create some with stencils (see page 99) or with painted borders (using masking tape, see page 102).

Another way to improve the appearance of cupboard doors and to set a style is to use decorative hinges on the outside of the doors.

This rich cream kitchen is livened up with blue sponged door panels, and delicate blue and yellow stencils behind the hob.

OLD FURNITURE

If you like to scour second-hand furniture shops and markets, and enjoy renovating the pieces you pick up, there are many methods of doing so. If you want to maintain the look of the wood, wood stains are now available in a wide range of colours. You can imitate the grain and colour of expensive wood on a softwood piece of furniture using wood stains or paint effects such as vinegar graining (see page 93). Carry out a test first on the back of the door or on a piece of wood that is out of sight. Work along the grain and try not to go over an area that you have already covered. This could lead to blotches.

On moulded or decorative areas, use a lint-free cloth to get the stain into the crevices. It is always better to thin the coats and use more rather than slap on one and find the colour is too intense.

DISTINCTIVE SHELVING

Shelves are useful for displaying kitchen accessories and providing an accessible means of storage for both the creative and the lazy cook. Some shelving systems have long traditions: pots kept high above the range, for example, and plates drained in slatted wooden racks. However, any shelf that is not enclosed needs a wipeable finish to remove the dirt and grime that is inevitable in the kitchen. You can either seal the shelves with a couple of coats of thinned varnish or use gloss paints. Always make sure you follow the proper procedure of sanding down between coats to build up a flawless surface.

If you prefer the uncluttered look, kitchen manufacturers have designed a cornucopia of fitments ranging from nifty corner cupboards and plinth drawers that make the best use of space to bracketed shelves that pull up and out with the electrical appliance already wired.

With the welcome return of wooden hand-made furniture, you can buy wooden cupboard units that fit in less orthodox places. These include corner cupboards and wall units that have that extra fretwork in the surrounds and they are ideal for dragging (see page 82) and ageing (see page 96).

This tiny vibrant blue kitchen is designed like a U-shaped dresser where the plinth moulding follows the work surface. Shelving provides storage for china, pots and pans and groceries. This is a kitchen where minimal effort is needed. The cook can stand in one place and reach just about everything – the dishes are stored in their draining racks.

The large modern dresser opposite has glazed cupboards for dust-free display. The woodwork is dragged in pale green and the worktop is of solid wood. This dresser arrangement is informal and adaptable.

METALLIC SURFACES

There are always some metal or ceramic surfaces in the kitchen, most obviously the worktops, splashback, electrical appliances and central heating radiators. There is no reason why a metal surface should not be painted in the same way as wooden ones are. Brand new gleaming appliances sometimes beg for a softening or a jokey approach. We are so used to seeing these appliances with their flawless factory-finish that any painting has to be done really well if it is not to appear amateurish and tawdry. White appliances look particularly good, and almost believable, when marbled.

Fascia panels made from the same material as the fitted units are one way around covering up appliances. This leads to a stultifying uniformity so a paint finish could be the solution. Radiators look stark left to their greyish finish and are better painted the same colour as the wall if you want them to 'disappear'. Alternatively allow them to become a feature painted in a contrast colour with all the necessary ducts and pipes frankly displayed.

Any metallic surface needs to be carefully primed so that subsequent coats of paint adhere to the surface or, alternatively, do not cause the metal to rust.

The visual effects in this kitchen are provided by shades of red and green, arranged in strict geometry with zigzags swooping around the room and continuing over the cupboards walls and even the refrigerator. Relief is provided by shapes cut in wood, painted and applied to the surfaces.

Metal objects often have sharp edges and nooks and crannies, and must not be overlooked when preparing the surface.

Before you start to work, remove any flaky paint and treat any rust with a proprietary rust treatment. It is a good idea to provide a key for the paint by lightly sanding the metal surface first, which also gets off any residual grease. Sugar soap is another way of scouring the surface while cleaning it, and providing a key. For unpainted metal, apply one coat of metallic primer and then proceed to undercoat and paint it as you would any other surface. You should stick to oil-based paints as water-based paints may cause rusting.

For painted metal, wash it first with soapy water to remove any dirt then with a rag soaked in white spirit to remove grease or wax.

EFFECTS

The choice for metalwork depends on the kitchen style. If the wall is colour-washed, then the same wash can be applied over a radiator to help disguise it. Alternatively, a fridge can be livened up in a creative scheme with stripes or stencils. Metalwork looks particularly good stippled or spattered (see pages 74 and 80), perhaps because these effects imitate stonework, such as granite and sandstone, so well. You can paint wood to appear like metal. Gold leaf or metallic powders mixed with a size such as pva give a gilded effect and you can also buy special metallic paints that give the appearance of metal.

Gleaming stainless steel is the principal material in this high-tech kitchen. The walls are painted in a dull olive shade, contrasting a matt finish with the gloss of steel.

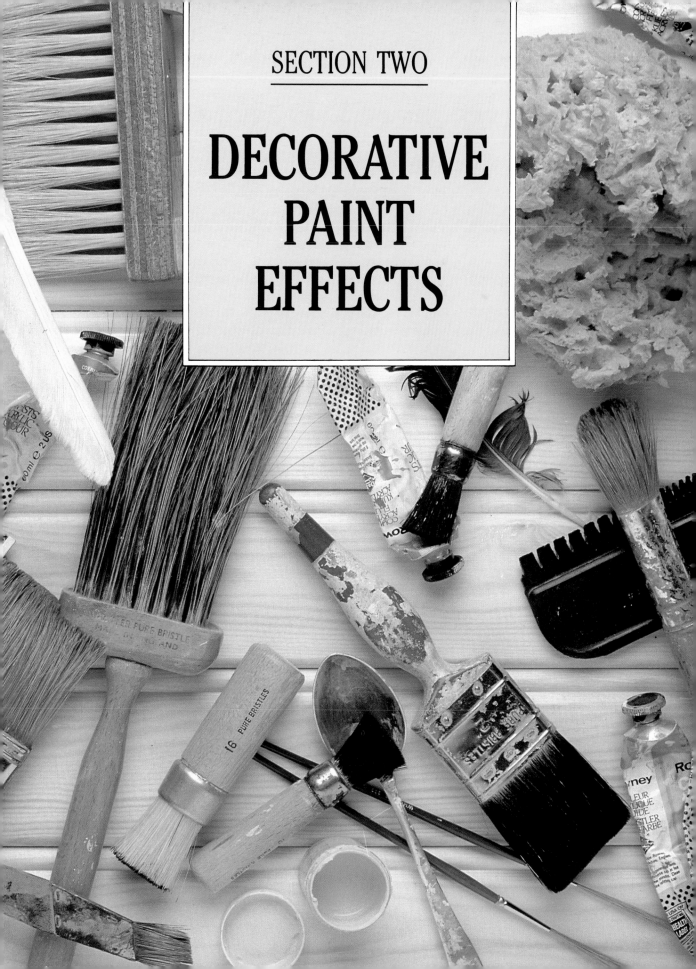

SECTION TWO

DECORATIVE PAINT EFFECTS

WHAT ARE PAINT EFFECTS?

Using paint and distressing it to give it depth or to break up the colour is a very old idea. The effect wrought by these methods can be regular or a fantasy, pretending to be something that it isn't: paint can be used, for example, to make wood look like marble or plaster look like metal or brand new tongue and groove boards can be made to look like weathered panelling.

A distressed surface is often more attractive than plain flat paint which in certain lights can show up all the irregularities of a surface. By breaking up the colour you can combine colour in imaginative ways to create co-ordinating schemes, a gentle backdrop or dramatic effects.

You don't have to have any particular expertise to attempt the fantasy effects. By keeping the colours simple and getting the feel of the finish, you will still achieve creditable results. The effect doesn't even have to be believable (you wouldn't then get any compliments for your handiwork). Try to copy the real thing and, after practising, you should be able to use this experience to get the finish you want.

Like any successful endeavour, you must have a coherent approach. Work your theme out first, practise on pieces of board or lining paper and then use these to execute the scheme. Keep careful records of all your attempts. Don't panic if your first attempt doesn't work: paint isn't an expensive decorating medium and there are other paint finishes that work wonders at disguising an inferior job. Most paint effects are very adaptable and, though you are bound to make some mistakes, look on these as experience. The sooner you start, the sooner you will become expert.

The traditional-style kitchen cupboards are dragged in blue over a white base. The mouldings have been dragged more thoroughly, so that the white base colour emphasizes the relief detail.

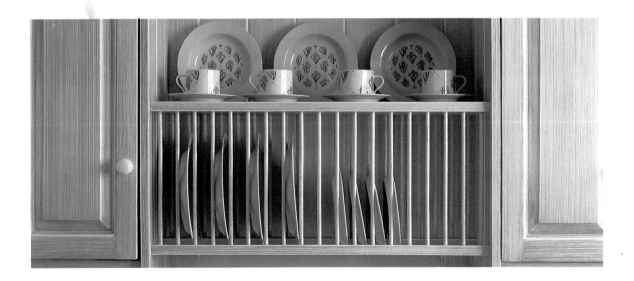

PREPARING TO PAINT

Painting is not just about brushing paint from a pot straight onto a surface. If you have ever asked a decorator for a quote and been shocked by the price, you may then realize how much preparation is necessary before any decorating can start. If the surface is not 'made good', all the effort will be wasted because the paint will probably fade or flake off within a year or two.

Taking account of the way you approach decorating is important before you start. The chore of clearing up, putting everything away and cleaning brushes can make the task awesome and not very enjoyable. So keeping all the equipment in a place where it is accessible and will not be disturbed for the duration of the decorating is a great help.

PREPARING SURFACES

Wallpaper Lining papers are purpose-made for painting over but if the wall is already papered with a good-quality paper, you can use this as a lining unless it is very boldly patterned. Vinyl papers cannot be painted over, but you can usually peel off the vinyl top layer to reveal a lining paper backing. Seal wallpaper with size before painting.

When applying paint to wallpaper, don't panic if the paper lifts. It will dry flat against the wall.

Plaster Preparation depends on what sort of paint you are using and the effect you wish to achieve. If you are using oil-based paints for stippling or dragging, then the plaster has to be flawless and smooth. If you want a more rough and ready look and are using emulsion paints, then as long as the plaster isn't flaking, the bumpy finish will contribute to the final look.

Large dents and cracks on the surface do need to be filled. (If you are using a dark paint, even small holes will be obvious.) Work the appropriate filler into the cracks or dents with a filling knife,

leaving it proud of the surface. When the filler is dry, sand it down flush with the surface. If there are any dents still visible, paint the area with a water-based filler that has been thinned to a suitable consistency.

After the first coat of paint has been applied, you will be able to see quite clearly any remaining imperfections. With a filling knife, go over the surface and fill any tiny holes. Dry, then rub down before applying subsequent coats of paint. Old plaster may need to be primed with shellac to protect it from flaking and to prevent the paint seeping in too deeply.

Woodwork If there are no flaking or thick layers of paint, you can work straight over the existing paintwork after first sanding it down to provide a key and cleaning out all the dirt and dust from the crevices. Sugar soap does the job well because it scours the surface while cleaning it. Treat any small imperfections and fill holes with wood filler, prime and sand down. If you are using a gloss finish, dents and bumps will become much more obvious. If the paint layers are thick and crumbling, then strip the existing paint down to the bare wood with a chemical stripper or a blow torch.

If the wood is new or has already been stripped, it will need to be primed before painting so that the paint doesn't soak into the wood and provides a key for the undercoat. Check on new wood for any knots, as the resin can seep out and stain the paint finish. Apply a proprietary knotting solution to any knots, according to the manufacturer's instructions, and then prime the wood.

Choose the appropriate primer for the surface. For example, aluminium primer is the best primer for woodwork in kitchens where the surface is likely to get wet directly or through condensation. You can also buy a universal primer that is suitable for wood, plaster and metal.

Because oil-based paints are hard wearing they are normally used on wood surfaces like skirting boards, doors and window frames. The flat eggshell paints are the most flattering; high gloss tends to show up all the imperfections. However, if you are more comfortable working with water-based paints, you can protect your paintwork with coats of varnish. The colours are certainly more subtle, and this may be the effect you want.

CHOOSING THE PAINT

Like many modern products that we take for granted, paints are the result of chemical compositions, so if the wrong paint is applied to the wrong surface, the reaction may be a great disappointment to you. For example, a water-based emulsion paint should not be used on a metal radiator – it may rust. Choosing the right paint for the job *is* important for a successful finish.

Paint technology has resulted in thousands of colours and finishes for all purposes – matt, semi-gloss and gloss, silk and eggshell finishes, non-drip and liquid, textured and enamel paints. You should be able to find the colour that gives you the look you want in a paint type appropriate for the surface and the task.

The undercoat is an important part of all paint effects. It contains coarser pigment particles than top coat paints, giving a greater depth of colour so the original surface won't show through. It also raises the grain of the wood ready for sanding. The first coat should be thinned a little so the paint flows and gives a smooth, even foundation for all subsequent coats.

The base coat is the coat over which the glaze or wash (see opposite) is worked: eggshell is probably the best paint to use as gloss is too shiny.

The fun in paint effects comes as much from the individual effect as from getting the colours right. Don't deny yourself the revelations that come from mixing commercial paints to get new colours. Although there are commercial paints where the colours are mixed especially for you, for small areas it is sometimes easier to get the right colour yourself and it is a way to use up left-over paint. This is particularly true of colours that may not be fashionable at the time.

Mixing your own base colour is only suitable for small areas; if you are painting the walls of a room, there is bound to be a commercial paint close to the colour you want and if it doesn't seem quite right, tint it to bring it to your chosen colour rather than starting from scratch.

When mixing oil- or water-based paints, choose the tones in the middle of the colour spectrum for the base colour; they require less paint to change their tones. The decision as to whether it is the right colour is entirely up to you; there is no absolute ratio of base colour to tint. Just keep adding and mixing drops or blobs of colour at a time until you have a pleasing result. Adding white brightens and black dulls (don't use black to reduce brightness, use a complementary colour instead), so these are other options.

To tint paints, use artist's oil or acrylic paints or universal stainers (see page 61).

THE GLAZE

The glaze or top coat can be a thinned oil- or water-based paint depending on the surface and the effect you want. Thin with water for water-based paints and white spirit (faster drying) or turpentine (slower drying) for an oil-based glaze.

The most effective glaze coat is based on a translucent paint medium, also known as scumble glaze or transparent oil glaze. It has no pigment. Because so many paint effects are based on the same principle – applying and moving paint around over a base coat – the paint to be moved needs to be slow drying to give you time to get the right effect. Transparent oil glaze is the best material for this. If you are unable to find any at your local store or by mail order (see page 140), then make some yourself with 500 ml (1 pint) turpentine, 300 ml (12 floz) ready boiled linseed oil, 200 ml (8 floz) dryers, and 1 tablespoon whiting. The dryers are needed because home-made glaze can still be tacky to touch after a week.

The colour is added to the glaze in the form of oil-based paints, artist's oil paints or universal stainers. The tinted glaze is then thinned to the correct consistency for the particular effect. For example, sponging and ragging need a thinner glaze than combing which is a more textured finish. The usual ratio is about 1 part thinner to 6 or 7 parts glaze. Make enough for the whole job before you start (see tables on page 00). Even though scumble has no pigment it will yellow colours. This enhances the earth colours but not the blues and greens. Even though your colour mix looks pale when you paint it on a test paper, it will darken when dry. Be conservative about colour; you can always darken it if necessary.

Oil glaze does need protecting and to ensure that your hard work is durable, seal it with a varnish (see page 61) and buff with wax where necessary. Always work with glaze in a dust-free atmosphere, keeping draughts to a minimum.

MIXING THE GLAZE

There is a wide range of coloured materials that can be used to tint a glaze of oil- or water-based paint. The scumble glaze can be coloured with egg-shell paint. The ratio is usually about 70 per cent glaze, 10 per cent solvent (maximum) and 20 per cent eggshell paint.

A basic range of artist's oil paints, when mixed together, gives a wide variety of colours – raw umber, burnt umber, raw sienna, burnt sienna, black, lemon chrome, chrome orange, yellow ochre. Artist's acrylics are mixed with water-based paints. Universal stainers can be used with both oil- and water-based paints but there is a limited

Two pieces of furniture combine to provide an interestingly shaped dresser. The cupboard doors are painted in green and brown and then aged with sandpaper (see page 96). One cupboard door is finished with a ventilator grill for storing bread, fruit and perishables such as vegetables.

colour range. Powder paints can colour oil- or water-based glazes.

If you decide to use artist's oils or universal stainers, mix the colour with a little white spirit and then add it to the glaze. Remember the glaze is supposed to be transparent, so use the colour sparingly, though it will lighten when you add the thinner. It is practically impossible to thicken a glaze, so add the thinners slowly and keep checking the consistency.

Test the result on a prepared board or lining paper that has been painted with the base coat. When you are satisfied, make a note of the colours and ratios.

The wonderful thing about glaze is that if your first brushstroke looks awful, you can wipe it off with a cloth and go back to mixing colours.

SOLVENTS AND THINNERS

These are used to dilute the paint to achieve the appropriate consistency for the job. Solvents are flammable so take care when using them and keep them away from children and animals. It is always wise to wear gloves and work in a well-ventilated area away from any source of fire. The most common solvents for oil-based paints are white spirit and turpentine. Methylated spirit is used to dilute shellac-based varnishes. Water is used to thin water-based paints and colours. Special thinners can be bought from paint shops.

ABRASIVES

These are used to give a key to a surface and to rub down the raised grain between coats to give a smooth, even finish. Sandpaper is the general term

The dining area in this Eastern-style kitchen uses many clever effects in both paint and fabric. The dresser is aged in grey and ochre, the walls are marked off to resemble slabs of soft pink stone and the area below the dado line is hung with fabric to add decorative pattern. A relief plaster moulding just below ceiling height and an intricate mosaic floor provide the finishing touches.

used to describe abrasive papers, although different materials such as glass and silicon carbide provide the abrasive surface. Each type comes in different grades, starting with coarse, through to medium, fine and flour. The finest has the highest number of noughts. Wrap the paper around a block of wood for a better grip.

Wire wool (also known as steel wool) also comes in grades, again the higher the number the finer it is. It is useful for rubbing down mouldings because it is more malleable. Wet and dry sandpaper is a good choice when you want to keep dust down and towards the end of a project when scratches on the surface would ruin the effect.

Extra fine abrasive papers or wools are the simplest means of ageing paintwork where a pristine finish is not the desired effect.

VARNISHES

A coat or more of varnish is a functional finishing touch to all paint effects in the kitchen. Kitchens and bathrooms are filled with steam daily, and with the inevitable splashes of water any unprotected surface will discolour, fade or stain if not adequately protected. If the paint finish is worked with a soft oil-based glaze, then this must be varnished to ensure durability, otherwise the finish will just wipe off.

Varnish also serves to modify the colour. Any oil-based effect tends to yellow with age. If you don't want this yellowing to occur, then tint the varnish with a little white eggshell so it turns slightly cloudy, or use acrylic varnish.

Polyurethane varnishes are all-purpose, easily available and easy to use. They come in matt, semi-matt and gloss finishes but many people don't like their brash glutinous finish. For an equally tough finish, try yacht varnish; it is particularly good for floors.

Emulsion glaze is the only varnish that doesn't discolour but it can only be used for areas that are far removed from steam and condensation.

Oil-based varnishes are the natural precursors of synthetic polyurethane varnish. Most are slow drying but give a very good finish and are favoured by perfectionists.

Acrylic varnish is a water-based product that can be used to cover oil- and water-based glazes. It is quick drying and does not yellow.

When choosing a finish, remember that gloss varnish will show up any dust trapped in the paint. So matt or semi-gloss varnishes may be a better choice. Use a tack rag (see opposite) to remove any dust between coats. To help varnish spread, dilute it to three parts varnish to one part solvent. The more coats, the better and more permanent the finish will be. Paint effects on floors need a minimum of four coats to ensure durability.

Colour and texture can be understated or bold. The bold approach favours throwing away the rule book. Using the colour wheel as a guide, or trusting your eye, you can combine unlikely and successful combinations. Texture comes with materials such as wood, brick, cork and rough-hewn plaster. Plaster can be tinted different colours and applied to a surface with powder paints.

APPLYING VARNISHES

Brush the diluted varnish in one direction first and then brush at right angles using lighter strokes to blend the brushstrokes. Then work on the diagonal to ensure a thorough coverage of the wood. The final brushing should be as the first to make sure that the entire area is covered.

When the wood surface is thoroughly dry, rub it in the direction of the grain with fine glasspaper before continuing with the next coat. A work surface, particularly one that will have water on it, will need several coats to make it impermeable.

To finish off, rub in the direction of the grain with steel wool and a wax polish.

A tack rag is a piece of clean lint-free cloth that has been rung out in varnish. It is an essential piece of equipment for paint effects. The rag is used to wipe over a sanded area to pick up any remaining specks of dust. Oil-based glazes depend for their transparency and depth on being see-through, and not mixed up with specks of dust. Store the tack rag

in a jar with a tight lid and keep it damp by adding a drop or two of solvent every now and again. You can buy ready-prepared tack rags or you can make your own.

MIXING CONTAINERS

Small saucers, plastic yoghurt pots and microwave cookware are all handy for mixing small amounts of paint or for decanting when stencilling. For large amounts, when mixing emulsion, for example, you may need to buy a plastic bucket or a paint kettle. Mixing glazes also requires a container large enough to mix one coat at a time. If the work is going to take several days, the container must have an air-tight lid to prevent a skin from forming.

To transfer paint from one receptacle to another, use either a plastic funnel or a ladle. If you are worried about mixing to a given ratio, use a spoon and wipe it clean after use.

An old wire whisk can be used to mix paints thoroughly. Scrap lining paper is useful to test out the colour and look of the effect. Alternatively, save old pieces of wood and use them as testing boards. You can prop them up in the room to be decorated and live with the colour and effect for a while.

BRUSHES

It is *never* worth buying a cheap brush. Good-quality brushes repay the investment if you take care of them. Cheap brushes are a false economy, as errant hairs appear in your paint work. You then have to stop to prise them off the surface and redo the area because of the mark made.

Decorating brushes have strange names; they fall into different categories depending on their size and the stiffness of the bristles. Always use the brush that is appropriate for the job in hand.

Decorator's brushes The best are made from pig's bristles. The most popular are flat brushes in sizes from 2.5 cm (1 in) to about 15 cm (6 in) across. Oval brushes are rare but they hold more paint.

Rollers As it is so difficult to disguise brush-strokes, you may want to use a roller over a large surface. These are either covered in foam or in a natural finish such as lambswool. A roller leaves a more textured finish which may not complement the subsequent glazed effect.

Sash brushes Small decorator's brushes used for woodwork (sash refers to windows).

Varnishing brushes These have more bristles to the square centimetre than regular decorator's brushes and they should be used only with varnish – any paint residue left in them will spoil your subsequent work. They leave a smooth finish with no visible brushstrokes.

Gliders Soft brushes that hold less paint, making them ideal for applying a thin wash of glaze.

Dusting brushes Used to stipple out any visible brushstrokes, these are sometimes referred to as softeners. The ends of the bristles are the part used to smooth the paint to a perfect finish. They can also be used to remove dust from the base coat before the glaze is applied.

Floggers These are special brushes with long flexible bristles used for dragging and flogging. The flogger is really the only brush that produces the desired result. As it is expensive, a dusting brush can be used instead, but the finish isn't as defined.

Stipplers Brushes with a wide end area used to remove specks of glaze in stippling.

Stencilling brushes Short squat round brushes with tightly packed bristles.

Fitches Stiff-bristled artist's brushes, they come in a variety of shapes and are necessary for painting and picking out details on wooden mouldings or on furniture. The round fitches hold more paint and are very useful for all sorts of work. Fitches can be used for spattering over small areas.

Artist's brushes These come in many different shapes and the best are those made from sable bristles. They are used for fine detail. Special liners are used for making thin lines; the bristles are cut diagonally across the ends.

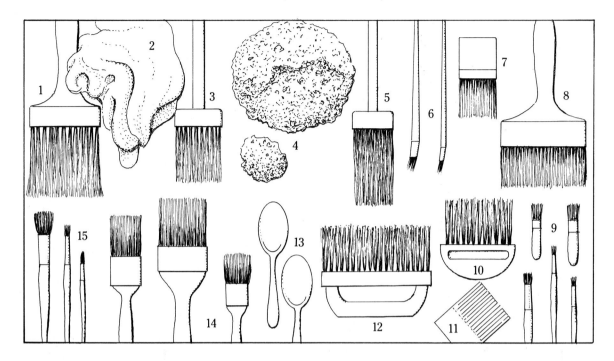

1 Badger Hair Softener 2 Cotton Stockinette 3 Hog Hair Softener 4 Natural Sponge 5 Indian Hog Hair Flogging Brush 6 Fitches 7 Mottler 8 Glider/Varnishing Brush 9 Stencilling Brush 10 Dragging Brush 11 Metal Comb 12 Stippling Brush 13 Spoons for Mixing 14 Decorator's Brushes 15 Artist's Brushes

To achieve a combination of painted effects, you need good-quality brushes and the right tools. The subtle marbling in this pink and white kitchen requires an artist's brush for control of the light grey veins.

Overgrainers Many different brushes can be used to reproduce the grainy look of wood. The bristles are divided up into a number of tiny brushes on the one ferrule to represent the grain.

CARING FOR YOUR BRUSHES

As soon as the work is finished, you must clean your brushes. If you have been using water-based paints, then simply clean them thoroughly in soap and warm water. Detergents dry them out. Lather the soap up so that you can get right down to the roots (the ferrule). Rinse thoroughly in running water, then shake to get most of the water off. Small brushes can be stored upside down in a jar, but bigger brushes are better stored suspended from a hook so the air circulating keeps them from mildewing and the bristles don't dry splayed out. To keep the bristle shape in the long term, wrap them in paper and secure with a rubber band. Stencil brushes and other round brushes should always be stored this way. Never leave brushes stored lying down.

Oil-based paints are cleaned off with white spirit or a commercial brush cleaner. Then continue as before by thoroughly rinsing in water and storing carefully.

If you are leaving the work for just an hour or two, keep the bristles moist in foil or in a rag dampened with water or turpentine (depending on the paint).

WOOD

Fashions for colour or natural finishes change all the time. The ubiquitous stripped pine dresser can be transformed with a dragged warm colour and stencil motifs. If you prefer the natural look of wood, there are many finishes you can apply to preserve the wood and decorate the kitchen. If the wood has so many blemishes that you need to make extensive use of wood filler, it is probably better to wax or oil it for the truly natural look. Your preference for a decorative finish has to take account of the raw materials you have.

BLEACHING

This is used to lighten the colour of wood or to remove stains. Use a proprietary two-part wood bleach and follow the manufacturer's instructions carefully. The bleach is usually applied in two stages; the first stage is a catalyst and the second is the bleaching agent.

STAINING

Commercial stains are usually labelled according to the wood colour they are supposed to imitate. However, you can never stain wood lighter than the colour it already is unless you bleach it first and you can never pass off a softwood as a hardwood because the grain will not be the same.

Water based stains – in crystal or powder form in bright clear colours; these are not as penetrating as oil- or spirit-based stains. You will need to apply at least two coats. The water causes the grain of the wood to swell so the surface must be re-sanded

This all-wood kitchen demonstrates the qualities of wood that make it such a favourite – the mellow tones, craftsmanship and the elegance of natural materials.

when dry. If the effect is still patchy, then apply the second coat. The stain may be less successful on softwoods because of their porous nature.

One way around this is to wet the surface first and allow it to dry. Then sand and apply the stain. The grain won't swell to the same degree as if you applied it to completely dry wood.

Spirit stains – come in both natural and colours that are not as vivid as water stains. They are best kept for adding a tint to a French polish. They dry very quickly.

Oil stains – the most widely used because they spread evenly and though slow drying, give the most even results.

Varnish stains – these can be oil or polyurethane based. They have a pigment in them so the colour and finish are applied at the same time. Because of the climatic conditions in the kitchen, the polyurethane stains are the ideal solution for work surfaces, shelves and furniture where wet dishes and food are left. However, the colours are thick and not so transparent. They usually fail to show up the wood grain, negating the desired effect.

APPLYING STAINS

Most stains can be applied with a rag. The absorbency of the rag prevents the stain being applied unevenly. However, for large areas, use a good-quality brush and work in a dry, dust-free room to minimize the chance of dust settling on the tacky surface during drying time.

SPONGING

This is the perfect paint effect for beginners. It is easy, relatively quick and, by its very nature, random and smudged so imperfections are hardly noticeable. The soft blurring of colour is ideal for inferior plasterwork. However, the simplicity of sponging doesn't reduce its impact, because you can create a striking effect with an imaginative choice of colours.

You can sponge plasterwork using all forms of water-based paint, making it a less messy procedure for the nervous beginner. The sponged coats should be thinned down with water. Two or even three sponged coats give a better effect than one, but, as with all these effects, try out different colours on a piece of card or lining paper first. Make a note of the colours and the ratio of thinner to paint for reference.

If you prefer a transparent effect, then use a tinted glaze for the sponged coats over an emulsion base coat. You can also thin oil-based paints with a solvent, particularly for wooden surfaces.

The essential tool for sponging is a natural sea sponge, available from health and cosmetic shops as well as from some paint suppliers. Synthetic sponges can be used but you must sculpt them across their entire surface to resemble natural sponges. They are cheaper and last longer – sea sponges become hard and shrink with use. When the sponge starts to disintegrate, cut off the shredded parts and use the new surface area.

The most usual colour combination is with a lighter colour as the base with the sponged colours in slightly darker tones or in a contrast. For example, a light apricot base colour can be sponged over with a pale green and a darker apricot shade. If you use a stronger contrast, the blotches made by the pattern of the sponge will be more separate or spotty, giving a less blurred result. The last colour sponged on will be the dominant one, so plan for this.

Sponging can be used to lighten up a painted wall where you do not much like the colour but don't want to start again. For example, an expanse of dull green can be sponged with a lighter green and a cream to change the concentrated colour to a more diluted one. Sponging is also a perfect finish for any area where you want a light touch.

The finished sponged effect is built up in subtle diagonal bands running from the top left. This needs to be planned beforehand to avoid clusters of colour or great expanses of colour-washed wall with little sponging.

Base coat: pale yellow
First wash: strong yellow
Second wash: reddish-brown
Third wash: brownish-yellow

1 Prepare the surface and apply the plain base coat with a roller or paint brush; allow to dry.

2 Using a stronger colour than the base coat, and a large paint brush apply the first wash evenly. Before it dries, quickly break the surface up with a softening brush or sponge.

3 The first wash completed, the broken-colour effect should already be evident as the pale base colour shows through here and there to break up the darker first wash.

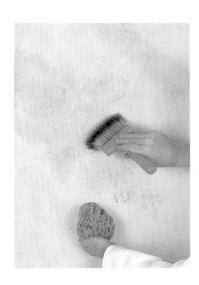

4 Dampen the sponge with water if you are using water-based paints (or white spirit if using oil-based paints), then squeeze dry. Dip the sponge into the second wash colour and, using light dabbing movements, sponge the colour on. At the same time soften the paint using a softening brush.

5 Stand back and judge the effect. Don't worry about any spaces left between the sponging marks. If there are areas that look different, sponge on some more base coat to dilute any more heavily coloured areas.

6 When the sponging is dry, apply a wash made up from the two predominant colours. Brush it on with an ordinary paint brush and break it up with a sponge or softening brush, working the surface as for colour washing (see page 76).

RAGGING

Ragging on, ragging off, and simply ragging, are terms used for a number of paint effects using a rag or rag substitute in different ways. Ragging on is a process much like sponging (see page 70), except the means of working the colour is different. The final effect is rather like light clouds of colour scudding across the surface.

The best fabric for the rags is a lint-free cloth such as cotton, linen or cheesecloth (old sheets or T-shirts, for example). One hundred per cent synthetic fabrics don't absorb enough paint so they are not suitable.

Cut all the rags from the same fabric into squares (about 30 cm/12 in), removing any long threads and seams. Like sponges, the rags will gradually become clogged and difficult to manage, so discard them and go on to the next, but do be careful. Paint-soaked rags are a fire hazard so they should be thoroughly dry before being discarded. Always work in a well-ventilated area, though not a draughty one or the dust will lodge in the glaze.

The safest colour scheme is one in which two tones of the same colour are used – a light base coat with a darker shade ragged over it. You can create a distressed effect on a brand new wall by using the rag to wipe off most of the glaze. This leaves a soft subtle colour with hardly any discernible pattern. A large piece of cheesecloth is good for this. To prepare the cheesecloth, soak it in white spirit or some of the thinned glaze and squeeze it dry, then dab at the glaze.

RAG ROLLING

This is a similar technique but the rag is held in a cylinder shape that is rolled down the wall. The effect is different depending on whether you roll the glaze onto the wall or brush it on and roll it off to reveal the base coat. This produces a repeated linear pattern that isn't boring.

If the base is a dark colour and the glaze lighter, this gives a good finish which has depth. Whatever colourway you choose, the results will be a delightful surprise. It is better to use an oil-based glaze because emulsion would dry too quickly and any joins would be glaringly obvious.

The finished ragged surface is given protection with two coats of an emulsion glaze. This seals the fragile oil-based glaze and makes the effect practical for kitchen woodwork.

Base coat: pale yellow
First glaze: scumble tinted with terracotta with artist's oils
Second glaze: scumble tinted pink with artist's oils
Finish: two coats emulsion glaze

1 Prepare the surface and apply a pale base coat. Allow to dry. Collect the rags, and protective gloves (advisable if using glaze and white spirit).

2 Apply the first coat of tinted scumble glaze with a brush using vertical and horizontal strokes only.

3 Start ragging before the glaze has dried. Holding the rag in the tips of your fingers, rub or wipe off the glaze in a vertical and horizontal direction. Rebunch the rag to prevent a regular pattern from forming.

4 Use a softening brush to soften the glaze further before it dries. Resist the temptation to retouch areas. Wait until you have finished before deciding about imperfections. They may not seem so bad when the glaze is dry.

5 Leave for two days before starting on the next stage. The first ragged glaze leaves a soft subtle colour with a barely discernible pattern. The finish becomes more subtle as you continue working the glaze.

6 Apply the second tinted scumble glaze coat as before, using vertical and horizontal strokes. Rag and soften as for the first coat before the glaze dries.

STIPPLING

Stippling is a subtle paint effect, giving a hazy finish that softens edges and harsh materials, such as metal. It can be used to age wood and textured surfaces by producing lots of tiny flecks rather like dispersed sprays of paint. It makes a flattering background for beautiful furniture or paintings. Instead of taking glaze off or putting it on, a bristled brush is used to move the glaze around. Often decorators use a stippling brush to smudge obvious brushstrokes. Here the entire surface is gone over with a brush to fade out the tinted top coat and leave a delicate finish.

Uneven walls do not stipple well; every fault will show through. It should be worked on a perfect surface with a glaze and requires two people to do it properly. Don't swap tasks part way through, however, as the differences in technique will show up. You have to complete the entire area in one go because if you allow the glaze to dry, the join will show when you restart.

It is safer to choose a base coat in an even colour; good results come from off-white or cream. This allows the base colour to show through the glaze, rather like pin points. The two colours need to be sufficiently different for the effect to be seen properly. If the base colour is dark, the stippled effect will soften its bold impact.

AGEING TEXTURED SURFACES

Stippling can also be used to give interest and character to relief surfaces such as anaglypta wallpapers and mouldings. The idea is to leave tiny specks of colour in the recesses of the relief surface. This may not be to everyone's taste, but it certainly adds character to brand new surfaces, such as a ceiling rose or dado rail, when they are used to decorate an older property or complement a certain style.

The finished surface has been covered with two coats of emulsion glaze to protect and prevent the yellowing that naturally occurs with a scumble glaze. The pinpoints of stippled colour merge to age the textured surface. Some areas are intense, while others have been wiped out almost to the base colour.

Base coat: cream
First glaze: scumble tinted with bright green artist's oils
Finish: two coats emulsion glaze

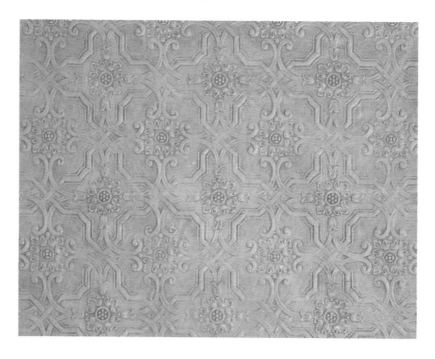

1 Prepare the surface – in this case, textured wallpaper – by painting a base coat of quick-drying eggshell.

2 Collect your tools. The stippling must be worked before the glaze dries. Using a paint brush, cover the entire surface evenly with the tinted scumble glaze.

3 With the stippling brush, work over the entire surface to build up the pinpoints of colour. If paint builds up on the brush, wipe it with a rag, not with white spirit.

4 With a lint-free rag, wipe the raised areas of the surface to remove some glaze and emphasize the build-up of colour in the recesses of the design.

Using your wrist and a light but firm touch on the surface, twist the brush after each stroke and before you touch the surface again. (Special stippling

brushes are available from hardware stores although a stencilling brush or even a shoe-cleaning bush can be substituted for small areas.)

COLOUR WASHING

Colour washing conjures up the beauty of old farm-houses and humble villas on Mediterranean islands. It covers imperfect plasterwork beautifully and conveys a feeling of rusticity and warmth to the most modern architecture with its patchy flushes of colour. Ironically, a colour wash can use the recesses of patched plasterwork to create a fantasy finish resembling ancient walls. Traditionally distemper was used to seal plaster walls: it dried to a finish similar to emulsion paint. It is this finish that colour washing recreates.

The technique is as it sounds – washing a surface with diluted colour. Traditional colours used are pink and blue over a white base but yellow, sienna and green look equally effective. Colour washing can be worked with thinned emulsion (the dilution should be at least one part paint to eight parts water), tinted thinned glaze or you can make your own glaze using PVA adhesive, water and powder colour. Each coat can be the same dilution or you can vary it to regulate the intensity of colour. You need courage for colour washing because the first coat will look dreadful but as more coats are applied, so the effect will materialize successfully. At least three coats will be necessary.

There is some similarity in method between colour washing and dragging (see page 82) where the glaze coat is taken off with a dry brush to achieve a broken coloured surface.

Colour washing is usually done with a wide soft brush. The more cross hatching of the brush-strokes, the better the effect. The strokes need to be random to avoid any hard edges and obvious brush marks. The finish makes a good background for other effects.

1 Prepare the surface and paint it with a neutral emulsion paint. Apply the base coat over this painted surface.

If you work a colour wash using a slow-drying scumble glaze, you will have more time for blending the colour. This is useful if you are using two tones of the same colour to build up light and dark areas using paint rather than many coats of the same wash.

Another colour wash method uses a large decorator's brush to work different stages. The finished effect is rather like the canvas of a painting with the cross strokes of the brush providing the texture. This should only be worked on walls where grand strokes will be easy to work. The best colourways are two or three tones of the same colour. If you start with the lightest tone you won't have to wash your brush out between washes. After the base coat is applied, paint the first glaze using horizontal strokes. For the second glaze, work a herringbone effect, building up the wash by painting in X-shaped strokes down the wall.

2 Apply the first wash using an ordinary paint brush and random strokes. You may need to work a small area at a time if you are working alone because the wash must be worked while it is wet.

3 Before the wash has dried, brush it with a sponge to blur any brushstokes that are too obvious. The sponge helps to emphasize the mottled or patchy effect.

4 Use a wet brush to soften the wash again before it dries.

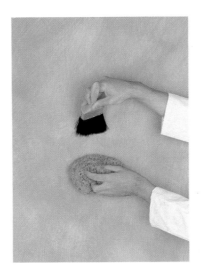

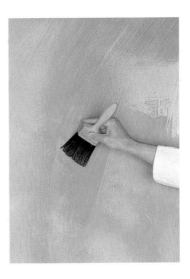

5 Using the first wash colour, apply a second wash in the same way as the first. Keep the strokes random, trying not to be too regular. Intensify some areas and fill in others.

6 An efficient way to break up the wash is to work with the sponge and brush simultaneously. This process must be worked while the wash is still wet.

7 Apply the third wash in a colour that is close in tone to the first two coats. Work the wash with the sponge and brush as before.

The finished effect below gives a fluctuating intensity of colour that enlivens even large, featureless walls.

Base coat: warm beige
First wash: sage green
Second wash: green-blue

Colour washing is a particularly good effect for disguising imperfect plasterwork. Here it balances the honey tones of the pine kitchen furniture.

SPATTERING

Spattering is a textured finish reminiscent of 1950s action painting. It leaves dots of one or more colours over the base colour and is a technique that needs some expertise and practice; it is most easily worked on a horizontal surface. The same technique can be used with a solvent to produce a watermark. With more confidence, spattering can produce a fantasy stone finish such as granite.

This is one paint effect that looks good starting with a dark base coat. A dark grey base coat with white, pale grey and gold spattering resembles stone; deep red can be spattered with dark blue and gold for a sophisticated finish or with black and gold for an oriental lacquered effect, and

Wedgwood blue spattered with black and white to imitate lapis lazuli.

The base coat can be an oil- or water-based paint, depending on the surface. Use undiluted emulsion, or a scumble glaze tinted with artist's oil colours, or artist's acrylic mixed with a little water. Even ink can be used. The glaze shouldn't be too diluted as you don't want the dots to run but neither should it be so thick that it forms blobs of paint rather than dots.

This is a very messy business so you must cover the immediate area with newspapers, mask off any adjacent surfaces, wear overalls, gloves and a head scarf, and glasses or goggles to protect your eyes.

The corner of a dignified Swedish dining room is given a dash of colour with spattered coats of earthy red-brown and bright blue.

1 Prepare the surface and apply the base coat. Gather the birch twigs together and tie securely. The undiluted paint should be applied more intensely for this first coat so use twigs of roughly the same length.

2 Dip the ends of the twigs into the first colour. Hold the twigs about 30 cm (12 in) from the ends and nearly parallel to the surface. Keep a consistent distance from the decorated surface.

3 Using clean twigs (tied so that some protrude beyond the rest), wait until the first spattered coat is completely dry before you apply the second coat, or the colours will run. As this coat is more random, adopt a flicking action of the wrist to produce lines and dots of colour.

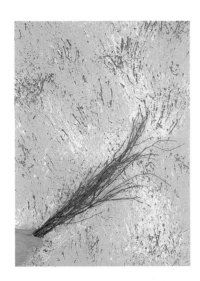

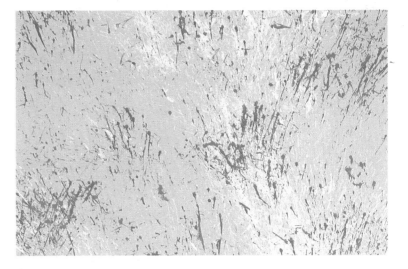

4 After the previous coat has dried, apply the next spattered coat with clean twigs and the same flicking action. Stand back every now and then to gauge the effect.

5 The finished effect has something of the look of an action painting. The neutral colours of the base are enlivened by the bright splashes of solid colour.

Base coat: warm beige
First coat: white
Second coat: dark reddish-brown
Third coat: blue

DRAGGING

Dragging is one of the best known methods of 'ageing' a surface with paint. Combing is a form of dragging (see page 84) but the usual method for dragging large areas is with a wide long-haired brush. You can buy special dragging brushes called 'floggers'. They are a wise investment because no other brush achieves such a successful finish. For furniture and small-scale wooden surfaces, you can use an overgraining brush (see page 66). As well as ageing wooden doors and mouldings, dragging brings a look of elegance to rooms with classical proportions and gives the effect of wood grains where there are none. Despite appearances,

dragging is not an easy technique, and to drag a large area like a wall, you will need two people because the glaze *must* be wet if it is to be treated successfully.

Dragging requires a slow-drying glaze such as a mixture of artist's oil paints with scumble. Choose colours that are close in tone; the greater the contrast, the more obvious the dragged lines will be. On door panels, for example, you can pick out the colour used for the mouldings and drag it over a paler background. Dragging must be done on a perfect surface; uneven walls are not appropriate for this technique.

There is a lightness of touch in this modern kitchen with its yellow sponged walls and pale blue dragged units. Dragging is a perfect finish for a brand new kitchen where you want the surfaces to look aged and mellow.

1 Prepare the surface and apply the base coat. You may find it easier to work with a partner if you are dragging a large area. One of you applies the glaze while the other does the dragging.

2 Tint the scumble glaze with colour and paint it evenly over the surface with a regular paint brush. The glaze can be worked for about 30–45 minutes, so cover as much of the area as you can drag in that time.

3 Use the paint brush to even out the glaze in preparation for dragging. Keeping your arm straight to maintain an even pressure, work in vertical lines. You may find it easier to hold the brush close to the ferrule – the metal part where the wooden handle and bristles are held together.

4 The surface is now prepared for dragging.

5 Drag the brush vertically down over the scumble glaze. Wipe any surplus glaze off the brush after each stroke. Line up the brush with a stripe on the last pass and continue, always keeping the strokes straight.

The finished surface dries darker than it appears while the scumble is still wet.

Base coat: brilliant white
Glaze coat: scumble tinted with blue artist's oils
Finish: varnish to protect

Combing

Combing removes the glaze top coat to produce stripes that can resemble wood grains or wickerwork. The tool used is a comb, and it can be anything from an Afro haircomb to a plastic adhesive spreader or special rubber rockers – wood graining combs. You can even cut 'teeth' in the edge of a rubber window cleaner. The lines can be varied depending on the way you drag the comb through the wet glaze – semi-circles, zigzags, criss-crossing lines and waves. Try out the design first on a prepared board or paper.

Combing is most successful when used for small areas, such as furniture, picture frames, boxes and trays. However, one large surface that can be enlivened is a floor. You can either comb in a natural colour and imitate the wood grains or choose bright colours for a modern style.

The colours chosen for combing should contrast so that the base colour can be clearly seen; the base coat must be shiny oil- or water-based paint such as eggshell to allow the comb to slide over the surface. For the top coat, choose oil-based paints or a tinted glaze, which will allow more of the base coat to show through. You can work with more than two combed colours: the top coat will dominate the effect. Dilute the top coat to a consistency thick enough to hold the combed lines, normally about three parts paint to one part thinner.

TRYING DIFFERENT PATTERNS

Work the glaze with the comb on spare pieces of lining paper to get interesting effects. For an angular design, work diagonally to make zigzags. You can drag long wavy lines over a large area, or overlapping fan shapes as large as the width of the comb. Combing a chequerboard in wavy lines leaves a pattern with wood-knot type marks, rather like the cross section of a tree trunk.

To make a chequerboard pattern, comb squares with the teeth vertically and then horizontally across the surface and continue along a second row. The size of the squares can be determined by eye or planned carefully.

The finished effect is protected with three coats of clear matt emulsion glaze to prevent discolouration, and finished off with a deep wallpaper border in a similar colourway.

Base coat: terracotta
Glaze coat: scumble tinted with burnt umber artist's oils
Finish: emulsion glaze

1 Prepare the surface and apply the base colour.

2 When the base coat is completely dry, test the consistency of the glaze on a piece of paper or board; it must be thick enough to form lines. Apply the tinted scumble glaze and then go over the surface with the paint brush, pulling the glaze vertically in preparation for combing.

3 Moving quickly before the scumble glaze dries, pull the metal comb horizontally across the surface at even intervals. The way you drag the comb through the wet glaze will determine the pattern. Hold the comb firmly in one hand.

4 The horizontal lines should all be worked first. Clean any paint off the comb with a rag before beginning each row. Drag the comb vertically while the glaze is still wet.

Combing can be used to produce a variety of patterns; two simple variations are shown here.

WATER-BASED MARBLING

With its classic beauty and cool, clean image, marble is an excellent effect for a kitchen. However, you need to use discretion when choosing surfaces for marbling. Start with something small, and keep it simple or colour wash a wall to reproduce a marbled effect. Marbling is certainly easier to work on horizontal surfaces and, if you want the effect to be taken seriously, avoid areas where the weight of real marble would make it improbable. Use the effect on skirting boards, work surfaces, table tops, floors and dado rails.

Books with recipes for fantasy effects give precise paint colours for the different types of marble. However, it is simplest to find a picture or a piece of actual marble and copy the colours and pattern directly from it. Building up tinted glazes gives the surface a cool depth that quite successfully imitates the natural lustre of the real thing.

Good brushes are important in successful marbling. You will need some artist's brushes, a softening brush and a natural sponge. Feathers can be used to imitate the veins that run through real marble. They hold very little paint, making them a perfect means of controlling its application. (Remember the veins in marble always run in approximately the same direction.)

Much of the success of marbling comes from working the glaze so that the colour is not consistent. Again look at real marble. The veins look as though they are deep within the marble, though some of them are mere dots. This apparent depth is what you are trying to imitate. In reality the dark veins are made when residue builds up in the natural fissures in the limestone's surface.

If you don't feel confident, draw a sketch of a piece of marble with pencil, shading darker areas and placing the veins and dots over the surface and use this as a plan while you are working.

The finished effect of water-based marbling is ideal for large surfaces where realism is not top priority. The finish nevertheless gives a classic quality.

Base coat: warm yellow
First wash: caramel matt emulsion
Second wash: reddish-brown emulsion

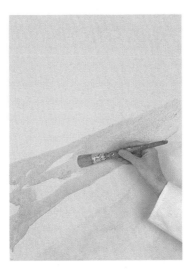

1 Prepare the surface carefully with vinyl matt emulsion paint. This water-based marbling effect is worked over a small area at a time.

2 Mix the first wash and apply it sparingly in bands using an artist's brush for better control. Here the effect is worked diagonally from the bottom left. The veins should run parallel and spread out from one another; they should *not* cross.

3 Before the wash dries, break it up with a sponge and soften it with a softening brush to give texture to the bands of colour. This step can be worked simultaneously as for sponging (see page 70).

4 Apply more wash to the surface and continue softening as in the previous two steps.

5 The first wash is now complete. The surface has been sponged in lines of glaze and softened to look like the natural fissures in marble.

6 With a stronger colour and an artist's brush, draw in more veins at random diagonally across the surface. Alter the width of the lines to imitate marble using the patterns of the previous wash as a guide. Again soften the colour with a sponge, working a small area at a time.

The finished marbled surface is not supposed to look exactly like the real thing. But the fluttering lines of rich colour produce a warm glow in this comfortable kitchen.

WOOD GRAINING

Wood comes in many diverse patterns of whorls, knots and burrs and in rich earth colours from the deep red of mahogany to the pale honey gold of maple. Successful wood graining can be achieved by combining a variety of techniques; it is a good idea to copy the patterns of a real piece of wood with earth coloured glazes and a variety of implements. This paint effect is not easy and it is better to have fun with it than aim for botanical accuracy. If you are planning to cover a large area, it may be wise to divide it up into sections and treat them separately. This works well on flat modern doors. They can be divided up into panels of *bois clair* with dragged mouldings.

The simplest method is to use a dragging brush (see page 82) or a comb (see page 83) or a combination of both – some combs and special brushes even imitate the whorls and grains of a particular type of wood. Done with steel wool, you can achieve an oak-like finish.

For simple wood finishes, use a dragging brush and water-based paints for the base coat and a thinned tinted oil- or water-based wash for the glaze. The best tints are the woody colours of burnt sienna and raw umber. The base coats can be yellow or pink shades for pale wood and brown or red for darker woods.

Fan brushes, flogging brushes or fitches are used for more complex wood grains. If the brush is held at right angles to the surface being treated so that the bristles splay out, the glaze can be worked into whorls or splinter-like brushmarks. Once the wood base surface is achieved, you can paint in the knots or brush with a special brush to get the parallel grain marks.

A special brush for wood graining is a pencil dragger divided into smaller brushes which each leave separate, distinctive brushstrokes. (You can tape three or four small brushes together to achieve the same result.)

The teeth of special rubber combs (rockers) are set so that they produce whorls as they are pulled through the glaze. After applying the glaze in a random way, run the rocker through it and then soften the pattern with a softening brush. By altering the angle of the rocker as you pull it along you can break up the pattern. Wipe the teeth of the rocker to prevent a build-up of glaze.

With these difficult techniques it is absolutely essential to try a sample board first, making careful notes of your colours and methods before starting on the real thing.

The finished effect is sometimes called *bois clair* – pale wood graining. It is finished off here with a garland wallpaper border. This is a good effect for imitation wood panelling between the dado rail and the skirting board.

Base coat: warm beige
First wash: PVA tinted with warm brown acrylic paint
Second wash: PVA tinted with brown acrylic paint

1 Prepare the surface and apply the base coat.

2 Mix the glaze and apply it evenly. It does not matter whether or not the brushstrokes are tidy.

3 Push the bristles of the flogging brush into the glaze, working from the base upwards to give a streaked effect. The bristles should splay out to allow the base coat to show through.

4 The first wash coat dries darker and the brushstokes can be seen as vertical streaks of broken colour.

5 Mix the second wash using a darker tint and, working as before, apply the paint and drag the flogging brush up the surface, allowing the previous wash to show through the streaks.

VINEGAR GRAINING

This is an old-fashioned method for imitating wood grain that takes just a few minutes. It works best on pieces of furniture, but try it out on an old piece of wood first; you might like the effect enough to use it on door panels. The glaze can be worked into a pattern with a rag, a flogging brush, torn cardboard or a lump of putty, which, when rolled around in the vinegar glaze, makes marks rather like the rings in a tree trunk.

Prepare the surface and apply the base coat of eggshell. Rub it down when dry and wipe the surface with a rag and a little vinegar.

Collect together the ingredients for the vinegar glaze. To every litre (2.2 pints) of malt vinegar add about 2 teaspoonsful of sugar and tint with paint or acrylic powders. Mix the colours with a little vinegar to form a paste and then add the rest of the vinegar and mix thoroughly. (A dark beer or stout can be used in place of the vinegar.) It should be the consistency of a thin wash but not so thin that it runs down vertical surfaces.

Brush the glaze on to an area of the base and wait until it sets – it should take five minutes.

Work the glaze with our chosen tool – a brush was used here – and make patterns by rolling and pressing or dragging the glaze over the entire surface. See how it looks as you work. Seal the graining with at least five coats of varnish.

An old cupboard is given a new lease of life with vinegar graining worked with a knob of putty. The rich glaze is tinted with powder paints to resemble valuable hardwood. The finish is given a rich patina with five coats of varnish.

Opposite:
Base coat: beige eggshell
Vinegar glaze: vinegar, sugar, acrylic paints or powder
Finish: acrylic lacquer

LIMING WOOD

There are a number of ways to achieve the bleached white wood reminiscent of Scandinavian interiors and the floors of old houses scrubbed clean with sand over the centuries. This effect is useful for toning down bright new wood, especially floorboards, giving a silvery bleached sheen to the wood.

The history of liming goes back to the sixteenth century when liming paste was used to protect panelling and floorboards from woodworm. It was again in vogue at the beginning of the twentieth century, particularly during the 1920s when the fashion was for all-white interiors.

This finish is usually worked with a commercial liming wax that leaves a residue in the pores of the wood, producing a smooth surface for polishing and a bleached finish that shows up the grain of the wood beautifully. It is suitable for ageing wood to fit in with a style of decoration that would be ruined by pristine new wooden surfaces or in kitchens where the style is pale and restrained. Liming is particularly effective on carved wood – for example on picture frames or turned candle sticks.

In the kitchen, you can lime new pine floorboards to make them look established. Oak, ash and elm are the ideal woods for liming because the open grain takes the wax easily. However, with a little effort, any wood can be limed, but if liming isn't done well, you can be left with the splotchy bleached-out pallor of wood that has been stripped with caustic acid.

WAX AND PASTE

If you are liming floorboards or wood that needs protection against water or wear and tear, you cannot use the liming wax because wax cannot be sealed with varnish. So buy a commercial liming paste and seal with shellac sanding sealer and a coat of varnish.

SIMPLE BLEACHED EFFECT

A quick way to achieve a bleached look is to paint the sealed bare wood with a white oil-based paint thinned with white spirit. Brush the diluted paint onto the wood and wipe off the surplus with a clean rag, rubbing off against the grain so that the stain stays in the pores of the wood. Another recipe uses raw linseed oil whitened with zinc white powder (Chinese white) and then rubbed into the pores with a rag. Seal with varnish.

This gothic-style country house kitchen in Sweden has its ancient floorboards limed. The austerity of the surfaces is offset by bright blue used as the accent colour.

1 The wood must be stripped bare before you begin. The boards shown here are new wood. Liming can also be done on wood that has been stained with colours such as black, green and grey.

2 Seal the bare wood first so that the liming filler only enters the grain and doesn't seep into the wood itself. Shellac sanding sealer is ideal because it dries hard in an hour.

3 When the sanding sealer is quite dry, open up the grain with a coarse wire brush. This requires quite a heavy hand if you are liming a close-grained wood such as pine. Always work in the direction of the grain. Any scratch marks across the grain will show up when the filler is rubbed into the wood.

4 Check the manufacturer's instructions. Usually a commercial filler is applied by daubing on with a rag. Work over a small area at a time. After the filler has hardened, buff up with a cloth stretched over your fingers. This removes the residue from the surface, but should not lift any out of the pores.

The finished effect is perfect for mellowing new pine boards. The grain and the knots of the wood are accentuated by the rubbed bleached finish.

Wood treatment: sanding sealer
First coat: liming wax

AGEING WOOD

To some people it may seem crazy deliberately to rub away parts of a painted finish and age new furniture but there is no doubt that you can introduce brand new furniture and wood into traditionally styled rooms with some imaginative paintwork. The timeless styles of the country, whether French provincial, English farmhouse, Scandinavian, or American Shaker, are all conjured up with a few essential elements – natural materials, lots of bits and pieces, and a timeless quality about the furniture. Deliberate ageing isn't designed to make the furniture look dirty or uncared for; quite the opposite. The effect should be one of cherished scrubbed wood and polished mouldings.

If you aspire to this style, then even the most faithful reproduction chair or table sticks out like a sore thumb because of its newness. Wooden panelling, such as tongue and groove cladding beneath the dado, or a year-old dresser, can be assimilated more easily into the decorative scheme with ageing paint techniques.

There is a combination of techniques for ageing new wood. You can start at the beginning and complete all the stages or stop when you are happy with the effect.

To age a brightly painted piece of painted wood, you can make the surface look 'dusty' with a glaze of a thinned colour wash using the first colour, or with another colour altogether, diluting the paint with four times as much water or white spirit. Use a dull tint such as raw umber. Fine sandpaper can be used to sand off colour on exposed corners and ridges or a light rubbing with steel wool will scratch and age the entire surface. This is the easiest method but it does rely on the accuracy of the ageing. Work on the areas around the drawer handles, the corners, the edges of the doors where paintwork would naturally have been scuffed and worn away with years of use.

1 To prepare bare wood, prime with a wood-coloured diluted shellac or French enamel varnish.

The finished effect can be protected and the level of 'deterioration' maintained with a coat of varnish.

Wood treatment: French enamel varnish
Special treatment: Vaseline or beeswax
First coat: undiluted dark green-blue paint
Second coat: diluted lighter green-blue paint
Finish: varnish

2 To pre-determine where the paint rubs off, apply tiny blobs of Vaseline or beeswax all over the wood with a small brush or with your finger. Make some of the blobs long by smearing the Vaseline down the grain.

3 Leave to dry for 24 hours and then apply the first coat of undiluted colour, making sure you don't remove the Vaseline. This coat should be left for a further 24 hours before the second colour is brushed on.

4 Now apply the second coat, this time diluting the paint half and half. If you want a more faded look dilute this second coat with three times the quantity of water or white spirit to paint.

5 When the second coat has dried thoroughly, scrape back the paint over the Vaseline blobs to expose the wood.

6 Sandpaper around the edges of the exposed areas with wet and dry paper.

7 Now go over the entire surface with the wet and dry paper. Vary the intensity of the sanding so that you rub back to the wood in some areas and only to the first coat in others.

A stencilled garland just below ceiling height
adds a decorative detail without slipping over
into fussiness.

STENCILLING

This is the one truly individual decorative effect. Though centuries old, stencilling is always popular because it is so versatile. It can be worked on everything from walls to fabric, from tin storage jars to stair risers. This is where the challenge lies: how to use stencils with elegance and subtlety. Try to avoid the temptation to repeat the same stencil on all surfaces from the walls to the furniture as this all-in approach only really works well in a child's nursery. In the kitchen you may soon tire of endless butterflies or flowers. It is better to start with a low-key approach and see how it looks.

Stencils are particularly welcome in a kitchen if there is no other patterned surface. With limited wall space, the area just beneath the ceiling is often the only horizontal run of wall suitable for a border. If you prefer motif stencils, these can be worked on a dresser, cupboard doors, storage containers, on furniture or on the floor.

One way to determine the placing of a stencil border or motif is to look at the proportions of the room and see what features are missing. For example, if the window is flush with the wall, with no moulded surround, a stencilled border will provide one. A line of panelled doors with little to break them up would be enlivened with a repeated single motif stencil.

CHOOSING STENCILS

The favourite stencilling styles are rustic or geometric. However, there are many others to choose from in the vast range of commercial stencils – baroque motifs and oriental designs that can be worked in sophisticated colours or folksy figurative shapes in primary colours. Commercial ready-cut stencils are sometimes illustrated in brochures that suggest colour schemes and positioning. However, making your own design is not difficult (see overleaf). You can personalize a

stencilled motif by outlining it freehand to make it look like all your own work.

Ready-cut stencils come in manila card, acetate or brass; acetate, though so delicate that it tears easily, is ideal because you can see through it, enabling you to position the stencil more accurately. Manila card stencils are made more durable if you paint them with varnish for protection so they can be wiped clean.

EQUIPMENT AND COLOURS

The paints to use for stencilling depend on the surface and your budget. As you need so little, the tiny paint pots sold for testing are usually sufficient but try artist's acrylic colours or mix left-over emulsion to get what you want. Emulsion is very good for stencilling because it dries so quickly and comes in a wide range of colours. If you are stencilling woodwork, it is probably safer to use oil-based paints for durability. After the stencil has thoroughly dried, seal it with a clear matt or gloss varnish. Spray paints can be used and stencil manufacturers also sell special stencil paints and crayons.

Stencil brushes come in a variety of sizes and you need one for every colour. They are stored with the bristles held together with a rubber band to keep the shape. You can also stencil with a natural or synthetic sponge, cut into small pieces and squeezed almost dry of paint.

When stencilling a large area such as a floor, you may find it easier to use a decorator's brush and a hard-wearing paint like poster paint. Always varnish floor stencils for durability.

To check for good colour combinations, make up a proof of your stencil design on a large sheet of paper and tape it to the surface to see how it looks. The background can add to the finish too; stencils on top of a sponged or stippled surface create a rich, elaborate look; with soft colour washing the contrast between the two paint effects isn't so great and the effect will be more subtle.

CUTTING YOUR OWN STENCIL

Designs for stencils can be found in magazines, on fabrics and wallpapers or in books, or you can draw your own freehand. If the shape you like isn't to the right scale, you can enlarge or reduce it on a photocopying machine.

There are some hints for stencil designs which will make them more successful. If you look at commercial stencils you will see that larger shapes are designed with interlinking bridges. These bridges can be just as important to the design as the coloured sections. So look at ready-made stencils for ideas on where to incorporate the bridges.

Draw the shape on to tracing paper or photocopy it to the correct size. To transfer the design onto card or acetate, either paste the photocopy onto the stencil or go around the tracing firmly with a soft pencil.

Whichever method you choose, secure the stencil firmly to the cutting mat or board with masking tape. Before cutting out, colour the stencil in to see how it looks and decide where any bridges are to go. Don't make them too thin; they may tear or allow colour to cross to the next cut-out area. Mark them clearly. Check that different colours aren't too close to each other.

Now cut out the stencil with a sharp scalpel and a steady hand. Press down firmly and cut corners very precisely; any extended cuts will allow paint to seep through. One way to do this is to insert the scalpel, hold it still and rotate the stencil around it (this doesn't work with acetate). Don't be hesitant; the lines should be clean, so make a strong movement without jerks. You might like to practise first with a spare piece of card or acetate. Acetate is not an easy material to cut, so you would be more sensible to start with manila card. After cutting the stencil, give manila card a coat of shellac to make it waterproof and more durable. Small tears can be

corrected with waterproof masking tape.

REVERSE STENCILLING

This method of stencilling uses a template to mask off areas so that the base colour shows through. It is a technique that works well with a paint effect such as stippling or colour washing. The templates are temporarily pasted over the base colour and then the entire surface is painted with a tinted glaze. When the templates are removed, the shapes stand out in the base colour.

Reverse stencilling is most effective when worked in close tones of the same colour. The templates can be small and simple – rather like the cut-out section left after making a stencil – a crescent moon, a leaf, a simple floral motif or a shell are ideal shapes to cut out of paper. Use cartridge, lining paper or thin card and remember you will need one template for each shape.

The planning for such small images is probably better left random, so they look almost as though they were scattered across the surface. Use low-tack spray adhesive to secure the templates on the surface while you paint. Wait until the top glazed coat is thoroughly dry and then remove the shapes. If you want a strong contrast, you will need a couple of coats, but a flutter of shapes gives the best results. If you are working with a large template, you can get good results with spray paint.

STENCILLING SMALL OBJECTS

Stencils can make a small object look hand painted. For example, the punch cards used in knitting machine can be used to apply pin-points of paint to objects in a symmetrical way. If you are applying small stencils at random to a curved surface, such as the leg of a chair, then cut the shapes from paper so the stencil can be wrapped around the surface while you paint. If you want a mere speck of a different colour for a finishing touch of, say, the buds of a flower, they can be painted in freehand when the stencil is dry.

1 Prepare the surface and apply the base coat. When this is dry, apply a colour wash (see page 76). This gives a more subtle background for a single colour stencil. Plan the positions of your motif.

2 Position the stencil on the surface, checking its position with a spirit level or plumb line, and secure it with low-tack masking tape. Pour off some paint into a small container and dip the stencil brush into the paint. Remove any excess on a piece of scrap paper or kitchen towel. Load the minimum of paint on the tips of the brush. If you load it too heavily, the paint will seep down behind the stencil.

Apply colour to the central part of the motif. As you gain experience, you will be able to shade focal points by building up colour in some parts of the design and shading away to the faintest colours in others.

Remove any masking tape and lift off the stencil. Never slide it; lift it off the surface in one quick movement. Wipe any excess paint off the stencil every time you move it.

The finished surface can be toned down by lightly sanding with a fine-grade sandpaper when the paint is completely

dry. Here the surface has been aged with a pale wash (see page 105).

Base coat: cream
Colour wash: yellow
Stencil colour: undiluted deep yellow
Wash: diluted creamy white

STRIPES AND BORDERS

A straight line, whether a stripe or a border that separates one area from another, is used in conjunction with many other techniques and often provides the finishing touch to other paint effects. Low-tack masking tape is a valuable material for painting all straight lines.

Painted borders can be used in exactly the same way as wallpaper borders, which traditionally outline a window or door surround, provide an edging for a patterned wall or follow the line of decorative mouldings. Borders at ceiling height help to reduce the apparent height of a tall room. In a kitchen a border can add the finishing touch to a row of tiles. Straight lines of paint are particularly useful as a means of altering perspective on a floor design. To ensure the paint doesn't seep under the tape on a floor design, score the wooden boards lightly with a scalpel along the edge of the tape.

A border or stripe can be painted using a paint effect. For example, marbling makes an elegant thin border on a *trompe l'oeil* panelled wall or cupboard door. You might want wide stripes over an entire wall – alternating bands of broken and flat colour or two completely different colours.

Borders are a means of outlining a motif – whether worked freehand or stencilled – or they can be used to produce a line that stands in for a structural feature, such as a dado or picture rail.

If you don't like the hard edge that a masked line gives, a very pale wash applied over the entire wall afterwards will serve to soften the stripes.

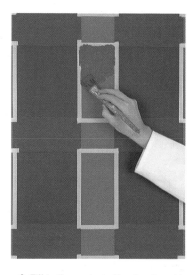

1 To create a tartan effect, first prepare the surface and apply the base coat. The base should be a lighter shade of the predominant colour. Subsequent colours can then cover it in one coat without the base showing through. Plan the lines carefully and draw them in with a soft pencil.

The finished tartan has a thin stripe of contrasting colour separating the blocks. After the first coats are thoroughly dry, apply the masking tape on either side of the original pencil line and paint in the contrasting line. It will appear paler because the base colour tends to show through. A wallpaper border with deep swags provides the finishing touch.

Base coat: cranberry red
First colour: rich red
Second colour: browny-red
Thin line: grey

2 Apply the low-tack masking tape with one edge butting up to the pencil line. Take care not to stretch the masking tape; this produces a curve. The tape will peel paint off a plaster wall if the adhesive is too strong.

3 Fill in the masked-off rectangles with the other colours. Here two darker shades of the base colour were used. The darkest rectangles may need two coats to build up enough contrast. As soon as the paint is dry to the touch, remove the tape with a steady downward action.

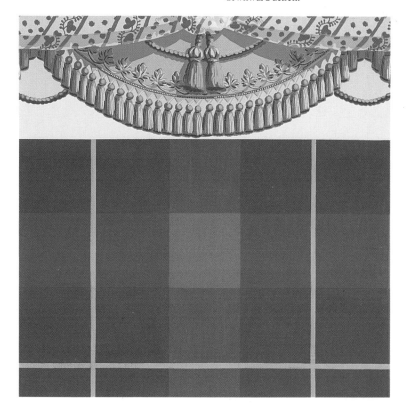

Low-tack masking tape can also be used to paint bands of colour on the mouldings at the cornice or dado rail. Here the dark green was kept quite separate from the pale cream with masking tape.

BLOCK PRINTING

Block printing is an ancient technique that can be used to enhance wood, plaster, fabric or paper. The printing block can be made from any one of a number of materials, as well as the traditional wood, including a potato, a rubber stamp, synthetic sponge, polystyrene and lino. The design is produced by either cutting away the surrounding material or fixing another material on to a custom-made block. If you look in antique shops, you may be able to find old wood-blocks. Special rollers with embossed heads were traditionally used to pattern expanses of wall, but a good-quality sponge roller can be used for the same purpose if you cut simple shapes into the sponge.

By its nature, block printing is irregular because the pressure tends to alter with each print, the paint will spread unevenly and if the surface for blocking isn't smooth the design will print only in part. These differences add charm to the final effect although if you design a large motif, you should plan where they are to go more carefully.

Some fading of the design is attractive, but over a large area it can be unpredictable. If the surface is fairly rough, use a sponge, which is flexible, rather than a solid block. You can always correct any problems later with a fine brush and a little paint. If you are nervous about repeating the block design across a large expanse of wall, you could print it on lining paper and then paste the paper onto the wall. Use fairly thick paint such as artist's oil or acrylic paints, children's poster paints or emulsion. The paint should be the consistency of cream.

Careful planning is needed to space this geometric block print around the cornice level. The block is made with strips of rope pasted onto a block. A blocked design adds the textural interest that you could never achieve with a wallpaper border.

1 Prepare the surface and apply the base coat ready for blocking.

2 This simple block is a square synthetic sponge. Decant some paint into a flat dish. After planning the placement of the print, pick up some paint on the sponge, check the effect on a piece of scrap paper, and press onto the surface to make the first print.

3 Continue pressing paint on with the sponge to make up the geometric design. Because the squares match up at each corner it should not be necessary to draw lines on the surface.

4 To tie in the colours of the finished blocked design, an off-white wash is painted over the entire surface. This tones down the colours and softens the edges of the prints.

The finished effect is matched with a geometric wallpaper border in matching colours.

Base coat: pale beige
Block colour: undiluted beige
Final wash: white wash diluted 1:5

TROMPE L'OEIL

Trompe l'oeil means to trick the eye and it is the phrase used to describe something that has a three-dimensional appearance without being three dimensional. It needn't be an elaborate work of art – like the traditional bucolic country scene viewed through a painted archway – it can be a couple of straight painted lines on a wall to imitate wooden moulding and to break up the monotony of a large expanse of wall.

Literally translated, most paint effects fit the definition of *trompe l'oeil*; dragging simulates wood graining; straight lines imitate wooden dowelling; plates can be painted above a shelf; a wreath of leaves varnished to look as if it has been there forever. You could paint a frame around a poster on the wall. Many of the ageing tricks used to give rooms a touch of medieval splendour are forms of *trompe l'oeil*.

If you are worried about your ability to paint straight lines or images, photocopies or cut-outs from wallpaper designs or borders are a quick means of creating a fake effect. You can merge pasted images in with the surrounding area by washing the whole surface with a very dilute wash of emulsion or lightly tinted glaze (see page 105).

In kitchens, there are many subjects for *trompe l'oeil* – pots and pans, plates, garlands of garlic and onions, and bunches of dried herbs.

The artists who painted the images on these two kitchen walls have real talent. Plain cupboard doors are painted to resemble brickwork or glazed cupboard doors. Large-scale pieces such as these are best left to the experienced artist, but if you use the real thing as your model, and paint the shadows as well as the shapes, you may be pleasantly surprised at your efforts.

DECOUPAGE AND FREEHAND PAINTING

Découpage is a French word meaning 'cutting up', used to describe a technique that was originally used to imitate the highly lacquered furniture of the Far East. The Victorians used découpage to decorate screens, tables and small boxes with multi-coloured images. The cut-outs are pasted onto the surface and then layers of varnish applied to seal the paper and produce a lacquered finish.

Découpage can be used in the kitchen as decoration on a wall to suggest a theme or as a focal point such as a fake bowl of fruit on a pantry door. You can cover biscuit tins, picture frames or wooden tea caddies and bring colour into the room; or use the heavily varnished design to protect the surface of a tray or table top.

The motifs can be floral or cherub decals, playing cards or cut-outs from good-quality magazines, postcards, food pictures, black and white photocopies from catalogues and pattern books painted to fit the colour scheme – all these can be used. You can buy reproduction paper vignettes of scenes and events or braid and tassel decorations in the neo-classical style. These can be used in a kitchen where a grand, more elegant period is the style or just as a humorous device.

FREEHAND IMAGES

Whereas a child's work is perfectly acceptable painted directly onto the wall or a piece of furniture, you may not feel so bold with your own work. Freehand painting does lead to comments and opinions being voiced and you may not be ready to face any critical appraisal. If you do feel confident, there are ways to ensure success. Good reference is a must. Scour magazines and books, wrapping paper and greetings cards, patterned china and furniture for images that you feel might enhance door panels or chair backs.

If you copy and enlarge the image and colour it in, you have the benefit of a practice run to see if the colours work well.

WAYS OF CHEATING

You can use a stencil to complete most of the image (see page 99) and then fill in the spaces and fudge the sharp outline with paint so it looks more natural, or you can cut out templates. Another subterfuge is to make your design in HB pencil on tracing paper, tape it to the surface with the pencilled lines away from you (the pattern will be in reverse) and then transfer the design by firmly going over the lines with the pencil transferring them on to the surface. The advantage of using tracing paper is that you can cut a paper pattern to fit the space and plan the scale of your drawing.

Successful images in the kitchen include the primitive bright colours of barge and Gypsy flower painting, the 'Rosemalning' or rose painting of Norway, and the still-life subjects copied from the paintings of the Dutch Masters.

Depending on the surface, work in water- or oil-based undiluted paints with fine artist's brushes. Lightly sand the surface to provide a key for the paint. For extra definition, outline the shapes in cream or dark paint and protect with at least three coats of clear varnish.

1 Prepare the surface, cleaning off any dirt and grease. Here the wall has been given a colour wash (see page 76).

2 Cut out the motif. You may want to photocopy it first to see how it looks on your chosen surface. Use low-tack adhesive to check the placement. When cutting out motifs, use sharp paper scissors.

3 Apply the motif to the surface using PVA diluted with water. This motif has been tinted with acrylic colours and allowed to dry before pasting on to the wall.

4 Paint over the motif with the PVA, taking the brushstrokes beyond the edges. The paper motif will shrink flat when it dries. When the paste is thoroughly dry, seal the whole surface with three coats of emulsion glaze.

The finished motif is now sealed on to the surface so that it will not fray at the edges and tear. On a larger expanse of wall, the motif can be framed with other motifs – ropes or garlands – or you can use masking tape to draw precise lines to make your own frame.

Base coat: brown-red
Colour wash: warm red
Motif: tinted with paint acrylic
Adhesive: PVA diluted with the same amount of water.
Finish: emulsion glaze

SECTION THREE

DETAILING
— AND —
ACCESSORIES

FINISHING TOUCHES

Just as you might combine accessories with your clothes, so a room can be given the right finishing touches with a few well-chosen details. You can look at the accessories in your kitchen as a reflection of your interests – a collection of jelly moulds or crystal salt containers – or as the visual link in the stylish kitchen – the dried flower display in the country kitchen, the 1930s china for an Art Deco style. These elements may be cliches but they help to complete the overall impression and create a feeling of unity in the overall design.

Most kitchens thrive on clutter of some sort. For the busy cook, the idea of diving into cupboards to pull out an unwieldy food processor or a toaster is inconceivable, although some of the more expensive fitted kitchens do have custom-built systems for the storage of heavy electrical items. However, what is a kitchen without its bowls of fruit, salt and pepper shakers, bread baskets or barrels and racks for wine bottles?

The accessories should be in the spirit of the style you have chosen. If you don't have a recognizable style, you can afford to be eclectic and collect things you like and then paint them. Choose colours that suit the room. Take a pair of candlesticks for example: if your kitchen is grand, then they could be wood grained to look like oak or aged by dragging or liming to look antique. If you have a cheerful family room, then red and orange or blue and green spattered candlesticks would look effective.

The idea of grouping things together is a good starting point. Even if you have no collection as such and you don't want to hide everything away behind cupboard doors, then group the items according to material or colour. Cork mats, wooden cutlery containers, salad bowls and wickerware stacked together in an open shelf provide a textural interest, albeit a simple one.

Accessories add to the mood but they can also be used to fill in a difficult space in the corner of the room, under a worktop or on a bare wall. These areas are usually filled in with towel racks, rubbish bins or the cat's bowl. However, they shouldn't be overlooked. This is where you can stack wine bottles or decorative storage containers such as wicker baskets.

This modern kitchen is decorated with accessories in the same way as other public areas in the house. This kitchen combines the essentials of storage with display. The arched hanging rack holds pots, pans, preserves, herbs and other odds and ends. Cooking utensils and *objets d'art* are placed near the hob; the plate rack is purely ornamental and food-related framed prints add the finishing touch.

STORAGE

Metal boxes, flatpacked cardboard containers and hat boxes are attractive and useful storage containers. They can be displayed frankly as storage for infrequently used items such as your very best linen or clean jam jars awaiting the marmalade season and they are the perfect shape for paint decoration. If they are painted in the same style and colours as the kitchen cupboards they can be integrated into the kitchen design.

Many kitchen utensils are notoriously difficult to store in drawers, and knives are dangerous left lying amongst spoons and graters. Along with the usual jugs and hanging rails, this simple ladder stystem in wood allows easy access to everyday tools and ingredients.

Many of the commercial kitchen ranges now include ingenious storage ideas. The cupboard opposite has pull-out shelves so objects at the back are not overlooked. Even within the cupboards there is a nice finishing touch – the eggs are stored in chicken-shaped wire baskets.

For storage of smaller utensils, why not decorate old chipped earthenware, glass jars or enamelled jugs and fill them with your wooden spoons or general cooking utensils? The utensils themselves can also be used for decoration. If, for example, you choose an accent colour of, say, green or red, cheap and cheerful green or red plastic handles may be the answer to brighten up the worktop. Even old tin cans with the sharp edges filed down for safety can be painted in co-ordinating or contrast colours for utensil storage.

Bent wire containers are increasingly popular for storing foodstuffs that need air circulating around them. Traditionally used as colanders and for egg storage or for garlic and onions, there is no reason why they can't hold fruit or vegetables. The wire base means that you can spot any decomposition before more damage is done. Wire is also used for plant troughs and wall brackets, cake stands and barbecue tools. The metallic finish fits well in a modern kitchen and its natural grey tones also go perfectly with French and country-style interiors as well.

The Shaker sect in America had the perfect solution for all their storage needs; they hung everything on the wall, usually from peg boards. Wooden peg boards can be extended along an entire wall or used to fill a difficult gap and treated to any number of effects – painted, distressed, stained, varnished, or wood grained. They can be hung at any level, even on the back of the door.

PICKING UP THE THEME

Collections can be shown off to advantage in the kitchen, especially if the thrust of the collection is something to do with food or cooking. Jelly moulds in copper, glass and creamware have long been popular displayed high up on a pot shelf or on top of high cupboards. Old carved breadboards, idiosyncratic coffee grinders, terracotta chicken crocks, copper pots and bowls, tea caddies and biscuit tins and metal kitchen utensils from your grandmother's era certainly provide talking points. Once you start a collection you can have many hours of fun searching through market stalls and junk shops for interesting pieces.

The talking point in this kitchen is the framed prints, paintings and china plates that cover one wall. This adds sophistication to the room, already attractively equipped with expensive steel and ceramic designs.

CHINA AND TILES

China is an endless source of visual interest in the kitchen, whether you display the china you use all the time or select co-ordinated china as part of your colour scheme. A bright room could take vibrant Italian china plates in different colours of the spectrum, for example. A blue and white china collection, such as the blue willow pattern, can be incorporated seamlessly into both homely and grand kitchens.

Individual china plates can be hung from special holders on the wall or on open shelves, the cups and mugs hanging from the shelf edge. On open shelves there needs to be some thought about what colours and shapes you display and how they are held there. A small tack driven into the shelf will hold one plate against the wall but it will not be adequate if you use the plate frequently. The usual means of holding china on shelves is either with a carved niche the length of the shelf for the plate to rest against or with bevelled dowelling nailed to the shelf.

The backdrop is another point to consider. Predominantly white china will not show up well if the background is also white or off-white. Experiment with coloured paper to see what background looks best. If the dresser or shelving system has no backing, consider using tongue and groove panelling to fill in the back. The panelling can then be left as wood or artificially aged (see page 96). Finally don't forget the lighting (see page 16). Another traditional finish is to stretch baize or felt tightly across the sides and back of cupboards as a lining. Felt is available in wonderful colours and with drawing pins or staples you can complete the effect in an hour.

A colourful display of hand-painted plates is arranged in plate racks beneath the ragged tongue-and-groove kitchen cupboards. This is a cheerful and successful display, drawing attention away from the plain laminated worktop.

Accessories

118

FINISHING TOUCHES

The shelves on dressers or large open cupboards were traditionally lined with paper or baize to reduce dust. This lining sometimes extended over the edge and this can become purely decorative. You can face shelves with lace, broderie anglaise, crochet edgings, or even wallpaper borders. This country look can be extended to the top of a dresser where a deeper pelmet of white crochet lace can act as a baffle to a fluorescent strip light. The same pelmet idea could be used along the top of the windows.

PAINTING CHINA

There are so many amazing designs in chinaware that you may wonder why anyone would want to paint their own. However, if you want to co-ordinate the china on a dresser or a centrepiece bowl on the kitchen table, unless you find some inexpensive china or pottery in a second-hand shop, when it is likely to be chipped, this will be expensive. If you should tire of the vibrant brights, then a change is not going to break the bank.

The quirky shapes and bright colours of these jugs provide the inspiration for the rest of the room. The chairs are hand-painted to extend the 'riot of colour' theme, while the white wall makes a suitable backdrop.

Modern ceramic paints are best used on crockery that you won't be eating off. They are non toxic but it is probably better limiting these efforts to china that you propose to use as ornamental or for eating out of, such as a painted fruit bowl or soup tureen where the inside and rim are left unpainted. Don't apply any paints to rims that you might drink out of.

The best paints to use are the special ceramic paints. Some are solvent-based and set dry to a semi-gloss finish without being fired in an oven. They can be sealed with a gloss glaze. Although long lasting, these paints will never be totally permanent as they are unfired.

The water-based ceramic paints dry with a gloss finish (in about four days) and they can then be fired in a domestic oven. Follow the manufacturer's instructions for firing because the length of time and the temperature is important to the durability of the paint effect.

Regular artist's oil colours and household gloss paints can also be used to paint china and ceramic, but for purely decorative purposes only.

There is a range of plain white china that is specially designed for decorating yourself. However, in reject shops and cheap china warehouses you may also find interesting shapes such as large jugs, soup tureens, deep bowls and quirky-looking teapots to decorate.

IDEAS FOR DESIGNS

Designs and colours can be inspired by the rest of the room or from many other sources. Spattering and sponging (see pages 80 and 70) are two paint effects that look appropriate on china, especially jugs and large platters. You may want to adopt a freehand approach with large stylized fruit and flowers.

To draw a freehand design, make the shapes with a felt tip pen or a wax crayon. Allow each colour to dry thoroughly before painting the next. Sometimes the design can be clearer if you paint around the shapes with black or leave an area of white china showing. There should always be a stripe between colours in a figurative pattern – look at examples of painted china in specialist stores.

The ceramic tiles on a splashback can also be decorated in this way. Obviously if they are already on the wall or work surface, they will have to be painted in situ with the less durable solvent-based paints. This won't be convenient for a worktop where there may be spillages from time to time. If you haven't tiled an area, then you can pick out one or more tiles and paint your motif design, say one that will be centred behind the hob, and fire the paints before hanging the tiles. It might be wiser to plan any decorated tiles somewhere on the splashback where they won't be splashed with water or grease. Water-based ceramic paints can be wiped clean with a damp cloth but they won't stand up to regular washing and certainly not scrubbing.

Make sure any surfaces to be painted are dry and free from grease and dust. If the surface is greasy, it should be wiped clean with white spirit.

The splashback is the perfect place for a centered motif of tiles. This example is from a tile manufacturer but you could achieve a similar result with ceramic paints and some degree of artistic verve.

BRINGING IN NATURE

The kitchen is the most obvious room for natural decoration – fresh and dried flowers and fruits and vegetables. There are also less obvious types to choose from. As specialist florists extend the range of flowers, seeds and other dried items they provide, you may find exotic dried seed heads and gourds. Mount them in a floral-type display, in a wall garland or grandly in a three-sided box as though they were botanical specimens.

There is no doubt that the variety of dried flowers and grasses makes dried flower displays an excellent year-round decoration. However, because of their brittle nature, dried flowers are better sited out of reach in the kitchen. Sometimes this means an arrangement like a garland along the tops of high cupboards, or along a beam, rather like hops decorate the beams in country

Tulips and hyacinths are arranged in a bountiful display to decorate a kitchen dresser. The flowers are placed in a container that is then hidden by a blue spray-painted basket.

The kitchen is a room of many likely floral containers. Old chipped jugs or those too large for everyday use hold instant floral displays of hedgerow grasses and poppies.

homes at harvest time. You can pretend that the flowers are being dried by hanging them upside down from the ceiling.

Round wreath-like displays are perfect for an austere corner, particularly against imperfect plaster where they look even more at home. Change the display from summer to winter and substitute holly wreaths at Christmas.

Think about the colours and textures of the display before you choose the ingredients. Arranging one yourself will be much more rewarding and you can make the changes through the seasons yourself. The earthy shapes of seedheads mixed with fluffy grasses and gnarled twigs would be appropriate for a modern kitchen while the pretty pinks and purples, yellows and blues of wild and species flowers are an essential accessory in the country kitchen.

TERRACOTTA

The warm sympathetic colours of terracotta pots and vases can be purely decorative or used in the kitchen for storage or floral displays. Unglazed earthenware takes colour well and by using masking tape or stencils you can create patterns and colourways on shapes as simple as those sold for pot plants and use them for storage containers or as ornaments. Garden centres sell large, elaborate pots, some resembling Greek urns, although these can be quite expensive.

Sun-drenched colours decorate the tiny terracotta plant pots so that they match the splendour of the centre piece – a hand-painted Mexican vase.

GLASS IN THE KITCHEN

Beautiful glassware displayed on pristine glass shelves looks magnificent as a display, sometimes teamed with shiny chrome. Glass looks good with dark granite-like containers – this can be achieved by spattering with grey, black and white, or even with specks of silver paint (see page 80). However, the kitchen is a difficult room to keep free from dust and grease and unless you have a glazed display case, the best crystal is probably best stored in the dining room. However, there are other less rarefied pieces of glass that can be ranged along open shelves.

Normal glass containers from kitchen shops can be used to bring colour into the kitchen. To alternate colourways, change the fillings in glass bowls or jars regularly as you might change displays of fruit – a subdued bowl of purple grapes and red plums in the evening and a brilliant splash of colour with oranges and lemons during the day. Large old-fashioned sweet jars can be filled with flamboyant boiled sweets in all their brilliant hues. If you want a more subdued filling, then cloves or cinnamon sticks provide sweet scent and texture too. Homemade or bought jams and preserves are integral parts of the farmhouse kitchen and you can go the whole way with dainty fabric lids if you want. Brandied fruits, herb vinegars and marinating olives or garlic are other culinary decorations, with the added advantage of being edible.

Large French preserving jars are used to store dried foods and these are often put on display either on open shelves or behind glazed cupboard doors. Incorporate them into your interior design; look at the colours and textures and place orange lentils alongside pale honey coloured rolled oats, and pure white flour next to cream ground almonds.

Coloured glass such as the carnival glass from the 1920s and modern examples of opalescent and painted glass can be used as a display. You can resurrect old pieces of chipped and opaque glass or old ketchup or pickle jars if the shapes are interesting and paint them yourself.

The opportunities for painted glass elsewhere in the kitchen are limited but if you have an internal window or glass cupboard doors, they may benefit from a subtle paint effect or stained glass (see below).

The traditional look on glass in the kitchen is frosting. This can be simply done with white car spray paints and stencils. However, spray paints do go everywhere so you will need to be assiduous in masking off all the surrounding area of glass and other surfaces. Work in a well-ventilated area because the fumes are most unpleasant. Don't use too much paint; the glass should only be slightly opaque.

Painting glass doesn't require anything different or difficult, but it isn't a durable finish so you have to plan carefully where you are going to put the painted glass. The paint finish is unlikely to withstand constant washing.

This pristine white kitchen is given bright splashes of colour in the cupboard glazing. Any cupboard can have its front panels replaced with glass and these have been designed with stained glass. The panels in the doors are softly marbled to give a shimmer of colour.

125

PAINTING GLASS

To prepare glass for painting, dissolve any grease with soap and water or a proprietary window cleaner and then dry thoroughly. You can paint on to glass directly with oil-based paints, French enamel varnish or use special glass paints. Spraying the paint is most effective because it is so hard to disguise brushstrokes on glass. If you do paint the surface use a soft artist's brush and apply the diluted medium in blobs of colour rather than in long strokes. To bring in texture, you can scratch into the paint while it is still wet so that the base colour shows through.

STAINED GLASS

Colour on glass is most often associated with stained glass windows. You can buy self-adhesive strips of lead to place around the design to emulate the leaded windows. Complete kits for making your own leaded windows are available from craft shops, by mail order or buy the lead strips from DIY shops.

    To make a stained-glass effect, draw the design first on tracing paper and check to see that it is the right scale for the position. It is wise to keep it simple; the shapes need to be large enough to surround with lead and be easily 'read' as a design. Tape the design on to the back of the glass as a guide. You can draw in the lines with black pen on the front of the glass (they will be covered with the leaded strips). Paint in the colours and when thoroughly dry, apply the lead strips.

Stained glass – whether an original feature, or as part of a decorative scheme – can add colour and interest, as in this pretty kitchen with its conservatory feel.

FABRICS

There are many opportunities for using fabric in the kitchen but you are constrained in your choice by the inevitable steam and dust. A kitchen is not a room where you would be likely to hang swags and tails at the window. The folds of fabric would soon be sticky with dirt. The best choice is the clean lines of blinds, either Roman or roller, and easily cleaned café-style curtains.

If the kitchen is just for cooking in, the windows may be better covered with shutters or Venetian blinds or distinctive bamboo style blinds. The glass is a cold surface and if the ventilation is not adequate, it will be covered with condensation which at night will look unattractive. Avoid this with improved ventilation and some form of window dressing.

The windows close to the hob should not be covered with any fabric that flutters and is likely to come anywhere near the source of heat. Blinds are the best choice. On other windows curtains don't have to be elaborate with heading tapes and masses of pleats, they can be panels of fabric, perhaps backed with a contrast or patterned lining and tied with bows or attached on rings to the curtain pole. This flat area of fabric is often enough to provide the softness of window dressing without the fuss. It is also the opportunity to apply paint with stencils or freehand to the fabric – ideally calico or canvas.

Blinds are the best solution for dressing a large window in the kitchen. This Austrian blind with its swags and frills is a risk in a room with such high levels of condensation. However, this room is large and well ventilated.

Café curtains are short curtains hung from a rod that is fitted half way down the window. They provide day-long privacy without reducing the light. There are many styles to choose from; the traditional type is usually made from gingham or similar simple cotton hung from a cased heading that is threaded over the rod or wire and then attached at either side of the window. The café curtains can be hung in tiers with the top tier opened during the day and drawn at night.

ROMAN AND ROLLER BLINDS

Roman blinds are the perfect tailored window dressing for most kitchens. They can be made up in plain monochrome textured fabrics for a streamlined style or in a bold pattern with contrast binding for a brighter, softer look. Roller blinds, made from pre-stiffened fabric and secured with a roller blind kit, can be individualized with paint.

The flat fabric surface against the glass is a perfect canvas for your painting expertise. Stencilling motifs, block printing and borders and painting freehand on fabric is within everyone's reach with fabric paints. These paint effects are best worked on natural fibres such as cotton, calico and linen; fabric paints don't adhere to synthetics.

Anything that is water repellent will be difficult to handle but you should always wash, rinse and press fabrics before making up to pre-shrink and remove any dressing. This does not apply to special roller blind fabric.

If the kitchen is large and the dining area is separate from the cooking area, then the possibilities for window dressing are more diverse. The styles of heading and the way the fabric is draped mean that any paint applied to the fabric may be lost in the folds, so concentrate on the edges of curtains or choose a small motif and repeat it to a preplanned pattern. You could use a stencilled motif as the edging rather like a binding.

A fabric pelmet above the window in the kitchen may be the only window covering. Pelmets can be made up from swathes of fabric draped over a curtain rod or cut from fabric and stiffened to resemble traditional wooden ones. Make the shapes interesting with curves or cutouts. You can even get inspiration from barge boards over the gables and doorways of old houses. You don't have to limit yourself to soft washed-out colourways. Be influenced by folk art and use bright primary colours on a neutral background.

CUSHIONS

Hard kitchen chairs are more attractive to look at and to use if they have a small cushion squab tied to the back uprights. This gives a soft base and the ties mean the cushions can be removed for washing.

The decorative finishes to cushion squabs are endless. They can be finished with braid or piping; frills around the edge can be narrow or reach half way down the legs. The ties that hold them in place are another way to bring some interest; make massive bows or use a long tie that has to be wound up

This kitchen abounds with fabric. The hard kitchen chairs are made comfortable with tie-on cushion squabs in gingham checks; the wooden settle also has a squab for comfort, as well as scatter cushions; and, finally, the windows are draped with a swagged pelmet. The casual draping makes the window dressing easy to remove for cleaning.

the back upright rather like ballerina's shoe ribbons. Commercial braids and tassels can be used to fit in with a more elaborate dignified kitchen eating arrangement. The possibilities of co-ordinating with the room and the table linen are limitless.

TABLE LINEN

Placing fabric on a table top is the simplest way to use fabric to soften the hard surfaces in the kitchen. The table that doubles as a worktop and school desk during the day can be transformed with a thick damask in vibrant colours for dramatic effect or a pretty lace edged linen cloth that is suitable for both a monochrome style and a pretty one.

Braids and ribbons and satin stitch in contrasting thread are just a few of the ways you can decorate table linen. Fringing the edges is even simpler, although the fabric must be of even weave construction.

For those basic kitchen buffs, fabric can be used as it was centuries ago as a curtain to cover up the area under the worktop. Traditionally the heavy cast iron sink on its iron base had a pretty fabric curtain below it. Gingham or a similar weight of fabric is the perfect choice.

An unexpected way of using fabric in the kitchen is as door curtains – an elegant alternative to glass in cupboards. These are usually made from muslin or lawn and secured with a cased heading gathered at top and bottom onto curtain wires that are then strung across the exposed area. Another method is to use a heavier cloth such as canvas and stretch it across the frame.

PAINTS AND EQUIPMENT

Always follow the manufacturer's instructions when using fabric paints. Some brands require fixing with a domestic iron. Some fabric dyes can be mixed for painting and there are stencil paints specially formulated for fabric. Remember to check first. Certain paints stiffen when dry and this won't be suitable for anything but a floor cloth or a wall hanging.

The paint can be applied with a stencil brush or a sponge or you can even spray it using a plant mister. As with all stencilling and painting on an absorbent surface, build up the layers of colour gradually using very little paint so as not to soak the fabric. Don't expect the first coat to be enough. If you are stencilling around a corner, you will need to plan and either place a simple motif at the corner or mitre the design.

FLOOR AND WALL CLOTHS

Patterned cloths make inexpensive coverings for an uninteresting section of wall. They bring in colour and pattern and, depending on their design, they can be the focal point of the room. Precious patchwork or lengths of batik can be starched and hung directly on the wall. Kelim designs with their earthy colours or Mondrian style primary squares and rectangles can be made from a couple of metres of cloth or you can paint one yourself on calico or canvas.

There is comfort and homeliness in this country-style kitchen. The tapestry cushions and the pretty tied-back curtains provide the individual touches. The cosiness is emphasized by the masses of pink and green floral plates.

Overleaf: Here is a kitchen in the grand style – relaxed yet civilized. The dresser is groaning with interesting china and the table is covered with a vibrant kelim for textual interest.

A painted cloth is an individual way to cover the floor. To produce a cloth that is suitable for the floor, you will need to stiffen it to prevent the corners curling up. It is also advisable to lay an undercarpet mesh to prevent the cloth from slipping on varnished floorboards.

The best fabric for floor cloths is a tightly woven canvas or deckchair canvas. The latter comes in narrow widths only. Calico is another option. First the fabric must be washed to remove any dressing and to pre-shrink it. Press well to remove all wrinkles.

The designs for floor cloths are limitless and depend on your kitchen style and personal preference. Stencils or blocks are a good technique to begin with but whatever you decide to do, it is absolutely essential to plan the design first. You can do this on a piece of graph paper using coloured pencils or pens or work on a piece of paper approximately a quarter the size of the finished cloth. That way you will get a fair representation of what the cloth will look like when it is finished. The edges will have to be bound so allow for this if you are centreing a pattern.

Designs that are spaced across the cloth are the best to start with; you can always build up areas as you go. The background can be painted using a paint effect such as colour washing (see page 76).

If you are planning to block print the fabric, divide the area up into a grid before you start. Decide on the spaces between each block and allow for the edging too. Now delineate the areas to be printed directly onto the cloth with chalk. This can be rubbed out later.

Use dressmaker's chalk or a light pencil to mark the guidelines of a stencil or freehand design and then stretch the piece of fabric out over a slightly padded surface – an old blanket laid on a table.

Using fabric paints, build up the colour on your design with a sponge or a stencil brush. Use the paint sparingly because too much paint will take longer to dry and you will be waiting for hours between coats. If you are using a block for a repeat pattern, then you will only get one chance so practise on a piece of spare fabric to check for the correct consistency. When you have finished applying colour, set the colours with a hot iron.

To protect the cloth, use a proprietary fabric stiffener or mix PVA adhesive with water to a ratio of 1:5. Paint or spray the stiffening agent onto the cloth and either hang or lay out flat to dry.

To finish off, back with a piece of hessian the same size as the floor cloth and sew around all four sides. Bind the edges with bias strips or use the edging braids that are sold by commercial flooring companies. These are available in wonderful colours. As a safety precaution the cloth should not be situated anywhere near the cooking area.

Scatter rugs make a kitchen look more warm and welcoming but they must be carefully underlaid for safety.

BASKETRY

Baskets hanging from beams or woven cutlery containers and vases for dried flowers are sympathetic accessories in the kitchen – their natural colours and materials never offend. Baskets come in all shapes and sizes and there are new innovative designs where traditional willow is woven in with synthetic tapes and dyed cane. Country kitchens often display the baskets that are used for everyday purposes, such as shopping and collecting fruits and vegetables from the garden, from beams or from rods on the ceiling.

Dried flowers are, of course, the perfect companion to basketry. You don't need to be a meticulous flower arranger; just group colours and textures and fill the basket to overflowing. Bread and fruit can also be served at the table in baskets and cheese can be placed on basketware platters.

You can change the look of baskets simply with paint. Ordinary household paints colour baskets beautifully. Apply the paint with a small brush making sure you get into the crevices. As a painted basket is more likely to be on display rather than used daily, you shouldn't need to paint the interior. You could use a plant mister to spray the paint on but, although quicker, this is so messy, it probably isn't worth doing.

Another method of altering the colour less vividly is to use a stain, the sort that is sold for colouring wood. This will be time consuming and labour intensive, but the results give a more natural finish.

The simplest combination is often the best – a container with fresh flowers. Here a two-coloured woven basket is used, along with the more traditional jug and vase.

Dragged door panels emphasize a harmonious blend of colours and textures.

TECHNICAL INFORMATION

The amount of paint you need for a particular paint effect depends on factors such as the absorbency of the surface and the weather on the day. The most important factor is how much you dilute the paint. Therefore, the following quantities serve only as a guide. They represent the amount of wall or wood that can be covered by undiluted paint.

Paint type	Coverage from 1 litre 2 pints	Special properties	Preparation
Water-based emulsion paint	14 sq m/ 16 sq yd	A hard-wearing finish that covers all walls easily. Quick drying and inexpensive, it comes in different finishes such as matt, silk and vinyl. The silk emulsion is washable. Difficult to wash dirt off this painted surface	Diluted with water, and coloured with universal stainers, powders, gouache and acrylics.
Polyurethane gloss	14–15 sq m/ 16–18 sq yd	A tough durable finish that is easy to apply. Wide range of colours. Needs a primer and undercoat or a previously keyed surface. Takes up to 12 hours to dry and the fumes are unpleasant.	Diluted with turpentine or white spirit, and coloured with universal stainers, artist's oil paints.
Liquid gloss	17 sq m/ 20 sq yd	A more traditional gloss finish. Needs more care to avoid drips. Requires primer and undercoat. Washes well and is durable privided the surface is well prepared and the number of coats are applied.	Diluted with turpentine and white spirit. Coloured with universal stainers and artist's oil paints.
Oil-based eggshell paint	16 sq m/ 19 sq yd	Hardwearing and good base coat for paint effects and gloss painting. It is the ideal paint for areas of high condensation such as kitchens and bathrooms.	Diluted with methylated spirit and turpentine. Coloured with universal stainers and artist's oil paints. Diluted it makes a durable colour wash (see page 76).
Primer	12 sq m/ 14 sq yd	Tough foundation coat (see page 57)	Not applicable
Artist's oil paints	—	Oil paint colours that mix with any oil-based medium to colour it. Slow drying making them ideal for paint effects. Dilute with turnpentine and white spirit.	These are successful paints for colouring oil-based paints. A couple of these paints and you can create most subtle colours for ageing and antiquing. Can also be used to colour scumble glaze, varnish, oil-based paint, in fact any oil-based medium.
PVA	—	A cheap and available adhesive that can be mixed to any consistency and used as a base for mixing with colour to make your own paint.	Mix it with water and then colour with emulsion, stainers, oil colours, powder colour to make semi-gloss paint that is not waterproof.
Powder colours	—	Ground pigment that can be used to colour almost any medium to make your own paint. Dilute with water. Can mix different powders together to get different colours before diluting or colouring other bases.	Use a a tint or colour to change the colour or proprietary paints or as a tint for scumble glaze and varnishes.

ACKNOWLEDGEMENTS

Thanks to Penny Bromley for providing technical information and checking the manuscript.

I am grateful to the following for supplying the photographs listed:

Chalon UK Ltd: 35, 129; Cotteswood Handmade Kitchens: 56; Grange UK: 17; Johnny Grey Kitchens: 33; Hygrove Kitchens: 12; Andrew Kolesnikow: 6/7, 53; John Lewis of Hungerford: 27, 130; Naturally Wood Furniture: 14; Newcastle Furniture Company: 120; Newman White Advertising Ltd: front cover; Robinson and Cornish: 50; Siematic GmbH & Co.: 115; Smallbone & Co.: 25, 43, 67, 104, 112, 114; Somerset Country Furniture Ltd: 47; Traditional Homes: 98; Elizabeth Whiting and Associates: 2/3, 9, 11, 15, 16, 18, 21, 24, 25, 29, 31, 36, 37, 39, 46, 49, 51, 52, 62, 79, 82, 88/89, 93, 94, 98, 102, 106, 107, 110/111, 116, 117, 118, 121, 122, 124, 126($\times$2), 127, 132/133, 134, 136, 137, 138; Mark Wilkinson Furniture: 26, 42, 59, 123; Woodstock Painted Furniture: 22.

INDEX

Page references in *italics* refer to captions

A

abrasives 61
accessories 113, *113*
  baskets 137, *137*
  china ι7, *117*
  dried flowers 113, 121–2, 137
  flowers 121, *121*, *122*, *137*
  glass 125–6, *125*, *126*
  terracotta pots 123, *123*
  wood 113
acrylic paint 58, 59, 104
acrylic varnish 62
adhesive, PVA 139
ageing 24, 74, 82
  wood 82, 96–7
artist's oil paint 58, 59, 104, 139
Arts and Crafts movement 32
Art Deco 113
Art Nouveau 32

B

base coat 58
baskets 137, *137*
  painting 137
beams *34*, 36
bent wire containers 114
bleaching wood 48, 69, 94; *see also* liming
blinds 127–8, *127*
block printing 42, 104–5, *104*, 135
bois clair 90, *90*
borders 27, 102–3, *103*
brushes 63–6, *66*
  artist's 63, *66*
  combing *66*

decorator's 63, *66*
dragging *66*, 82
dusting (softener) 63, *66*
fan 90
fitch 63, *66*, 90
flogger 63, *66*, 82, 90, 92
glider 63, *66*
mottler *66*
overgrainer 66, 68
pencil dragger 90
sash 63
softener *see* dustring
stencilling 63, *66*, 99
stippler 63, *66*
varnishing 45, 63, *66*

C

ceilings *18*, 20, 24, 26, 27, 34, 74
  beams *34*, 36
ceramic paint 119
ceramic tiles 38, 43, 120, *120*
chair rail *see* dado
chairs *119*
children in the kitchen 10, 14, *14*
china
  displaying 117, *117*
  painting 119–20
colour 19–25
  choosing 19, 20, 29
  psychology of 19–20
  understanding 19, *19*, *20*, *21*
colour scheme, planning 24
colour washing 26, 34, 76–9, *78*
colour wheel 19, *19*, *20*, *21*, 62
combing 24, 84–5, *84*
containers 113–14, *114*
contemporary style 32, *33*
cork tiling *39*
cornice 27, 103, *104*
country style *see* farmhouse style

cupboards 48, 51, 56, *69*, *93*, *114*
curtains 127, 128, *128*, *131*
cushions 14, 128–31, *128*, *131*

D

dado 27, 38, 74, 86, 102, 103
découpage 108–9
dining area 10, 13, *13*, 17, 39, *61*
distressing 38, 56, 72
dragging *56*, 76, 82–3, *82*
drawing a plan 41
dressers 33, 47–8, *47*, *51*, 69, 96
dried flower arrangements 113, 121–2, 137

E

Eastern style *61*
eggshell, oil-based paint 58, 139
emulsion glaze 61, *72*, *74*
emulsion paint, water-based 58, 70, 76, 99, 139
equipment
  for paint effects
    brushes 63–6
    containers 63
    tack rag 62–3
  for stencilling 99–100

F

fabrics 13, 127–35, *128*
  blinds 127–8, *127*
  curtains 127, 128, *128*, *131*
  cushions 14, 128–31, *128*, *131*
  floor covering 131–5, *135*